Trade—the Engine
of Growth in East Asia

Trade—the Engine of Growth in East Asia

Peter C.Y. Chow

Mitchell H. Kellman

New York   Oxford
OXFORD UNIVERSITY PRESS
1993

Oxford University Press

Oxford   New York   Toronto
Delhi   Bombay   Calcutta   Madras   Karachi
Kuala Lumpur   Singapore   Hong Kong   Tokyo
Nairobi   Dar es Salaam   Cape Town
Melbourne   Auckland   Madrid

and associated companies in
Berlin   Ibadan

Copyright © 1993 by Oxford University Press, Inc.

Published by Oxford University Press, Inc.
200 Madison Avenue, New York, New York 10016

Library of Congress Cataloging-in-Publication Data
Chow, Peter C. Y.
Trade, the engine of growth in East Asia / by Peter C. Y. Chow and Mitchell H. Kellman.
p. cm.   Includes bibliographical references and index.
ISBN 0-19-507895-0
1. East Asia—Commerce—History.
2. Exports—East Asia.
I. Kellman, Mitchell H.   II. Title.
HF3820.5.C48   1993
382'.0951—dc20
92-27965

9 8 7 6 5 4 3 2 1

Printed in the United States of America
on acid-free paper

In Memory of Irving B. Kravis

Preface

The four East Asian newly industrializing countries (NICs)—Hong Kong, Korea, Singapore, and Taiwan—succeeded in defying the vicious circle of poverty in the last quarter of this century and emerged as dynamic and rapidly growing open economies. Their success was so remarkable that it has generated a series of heated debates as to whether their development experience might be replicated by other developing countries.

The aim of this book is to reveal the sources of economic growth by analyzing the underlying mechanisms and interrelationships of this export success. We begin our analysis by utilizing the concept of revealed comparative advantage. Using Japan's trade performance as a benchmark, we examine whether the four NICs have gained on or fallen further behind Japan.

The trade patterns of the four East Asian NICs are carefully examined using a unique set of consistent trade data spanning a full twenty-five years, from the early "take-off" period of the mid-1960s, to the early 1990s. The export performance of each NIC is compared with that of the other as well as with that of Japan. The major OECD markets—the United States, the EC, and Japan—are examined successively. The responsiveness of their exports to external factors (e.g., world demand, trade protection patterns) as well as internal factors is studied. Not only are detailed product groups examined but such economic factors as specific product characteristics and embodied factor contents are explored. Economic theories, both classic and modern, are utilized to place the observed developments in perspective and to provide a sensible framework for understanding the "miracle of the NICs." The important issues of intra-industry trade and NIC import–export relationships are examined, and imports and exports of specific products are forecast.

We wish to thank the members of the Economics Discussion Seminar of the Economics Department at The City College of the City University of New York and the Seminar on Applied Economics at the Graduate Center, CUNY, for useful input. In addition, we wish to thank Bob Lipsey at the National Bureau of Economic Research and Ramon Myers at the Hoover Institution for helpful comments on earlier drafts of this book. Thanks also go to the anonymous readers at Oxford University

Press. Of course, the usual caveat applies: the final form of this book is based solely on our own decisions.

We also wish to express our gratitude to the Schwager Fund, the PSC-CUNY Research Award Program for financial support. Moreover, we fully acknowledge that without the assistance of the Pacific Cultural Foundation this book could not have been completed. Again, the views expressed in this book are ours alone.

Finally, we must acknowledge the tireless and capable research efforts of Mr. Deogjin Jang.

New York   P.C.Y.C.
July 1992   M.H.K.

Contents

8. The Comparative Homogeneity of the East Asian NIC Exports of Similar Manufactures, 113

9. Intra-Industry Trade: Diversification Versus Specialization, 124

10. The Next-Tier NICs: Tomorrow's Miracles? 145

11. Prospects in OECD Markets, 153

Trade—the Engine
of Growth in East Asia

1

Anatomy of Success

Spectacular economic performance in East Asia has had a profound influence on economic development and the world economy in the past quarter century. Rapid economic growth and the accompanying expansion of exports in Hong Kong, South Korea (henceforth Korea), Taiwan, and Singapore in the past two and a half decades have succeeded in defying the vicious circle of poverty in the post–World War II era. This success story is of great interest not only to development economists but also to political leaders and policymakers who are concerned with economic development.

As Anne Krueger pointed out, "[They] have demonstrated that poor societies can substantially transform their economies and alter their prospects. They have also demonstrated that rapid growth can be consistent with rapidly rising living standards for the poorest segments. As such, their experience provides a basis for optimism about future prospects of developing areas where authorities are committed to raising living standards of the population."[1] In this book we offer several explanations for this success.

Following in the footsteps of Japan, the four newly industrializing countries (NICs)—Hong Kong, Korea, Taiwan, and Singapore—have been extremely successful in adopting export-oriented policies to stimulate their economic growth and industrial development. As evidenced by the statistics of the International Monetary Fund (IMF) and the Organization of Economic Cooperation and Development (OECD), the share of their exports in world trade has more than doubled between the mid-1960s and the 1980s. The momentum of their export growth weathered bad as well as good times with unexpected resilience and durability. During the prosperous 1960s, all of the East Asian NICs enjoyed high economic growth rates, typically in double digits—a record considerably higher than any other region of the world. During the oil-shocked 1970s, amid world recession and the apparent collapse of their major industrialized markets, the NICs maintained a satisfactory performance of 6% to 8% growth. Their economic performance not only exceeded the average of the mature economies in the OECD countries; it also exceeded those of the upper-middle-income countries—the country group to which they belong, according to the criteria of the World Bank.

Table 1.1 indicates the average annual growth rates of gross domestic product

3

Table 1.1 Selected Economic Indicators for the NICs' Average Annual Growth Rate (%)

	GDP		Export		Import	
	1965–80	1980–89	1965–80	1980–89	1965–80	1980–89
Hong Kong	8.6	7.1	9.1	6.2	8.3	11.0
Korea	9.9	9.7	27.2	13.8	15.2	10.4
Singapore	10.0	6.1	4.7	8.1	7.0	5.8
Taiwan	9.9	8.0	15.6	13.4	12.2	9.6
Japan	6.6	4.0	11.4	4.6	4.9	5.4
OECD	3.8	3.0	7.3	4.1	4.2	5.1
Upper-middle-income countries	6.8	3.2	8.5	5.7	5.8	1.6

Sources: World Development Report, 1991 (Washington, D.C.: World Bank); Taiwan Statistical Data Book, 1990 (Taiwan: CEPD).

(GDP), exports, and imports of the NICs. For comparison', the figures for Japan, OECD, and other upper-middle-income countries are also provided.

EXPORT EXPANSION AND INDUSTRIALIZATION

Economic growth in these countries was associated with and "driven" by the twin processes of industrialization and export expansion.[2] In the early 1950s agricultural commodities accounted for more than 90% of Taiwanese exports. By 1990 the share of agricultural commodities from Taiwan had dropped to less than 10% while that of manufactured products accounted for more than 90% of total Taiwanese exports. At the end of the Korean conflict in the mid-1950s, when the expansion of Korean exports began, wigs made from human hair became the first major successful export item. Today, Korean automobiles and computers flood the United States and other OECD markets. The same phenomenon typified the experience of Singapore and Hong Kong. The two city-states, possessing virtually no natural resources, overcame this disability by first developing labor-intensive manufactured products in the 1960s, then gradually promoting more technology-intensive products in the 1970s after the first oil shock. Their success stories established a new conventional wisdom in the area of trade and development, highlighting the possibility for developing countries to simultaneously promote export growth and industrial development. Table 1.2 indicates the structural transformation of the economies in the NICs; Table 1.3 illustrates the shift of the commodity composition of their exports.

From Table 1.2 it is clear that the economic structures in Korea and Taiwan were substantially transformed from an agrarian base to economies concentrated in secondary and tertiary industries. The city-state of Hong Kong also shifted toward a predominance of services as its exports surged in the world market. From Table 1.3 it is clear that during that same period the commodity composition of exports in the NICs, except for Hong Kong, continually shifted from a predominance of primary commodities to more technology-intensive products such as machinery and transport equipment along with other manufactured products. Peter Chow has demonstrated, through the use of rigorous econometric techniques, that the unique pattern

Table 1.2   Distribution of NICs' Gross Domestic Products (%)

	Agriculture		Industry		Manufacturing		Services	
	1965	1989	1965	1989	1965	1989	1965	1989
Hong Kong	2	0	40	28	24	21	58	72
Korea	38	10	25	44	18	26	37	46
Singapore	3	0	24	37	15	26	74	63
Taiwan	27	6	29	44	20	36	44	51

Sources: *World Development Report, 1991* (Washington, D.C.: World Bank); *Taiwan Statistical Data Book, 1990* (Taiwan: CEDP).

Table 1.3   Product Structure of NIC Merchandise Exports

	Fuels, Minerals, Metals		Other Primary Commodities		Machinery Transport Equipment		Other Manufacturing		Textile Clothing	
	1965	1989	1965	1989	1965	1989	1965	1989	1965	1989
Hong Kong	1	1	5	2	7	23	87	73	52	39
Korea	15	2	34	15	3	19	58	59	24	29
Singapore	21	18	44	9	10	47	24	26	6	5
Taiwan	1	0	54	5	4	38	15	35	26	22

Sources: *World Development Report, 1991* (Washington, D.C.: World Bank); *Taiwan Statistical Data Book, 1990* (Taiwan: CEPD).
Note: Product classification for Taiwan may not be totally consistent with other countries.

of simultaneous development of industrialization and compositional shift of exports in the Asian NICs represents a reciprocal, bidirectional causality.[3]

TRADE AS AN ENGINE OF SUCCESS IN THE NICS

The success of the NICs, individually or collectively, is documented in a voluminous literature.[4] Some scholars explain the success by focusing on historical and external political factors such as the role of Japan's colonial policies in Korea and Taiwan,[5] or the contributions of U.S. aid and foreign capital in promoting economic development in these countries.[6] Others tend to focus on institutional aspects of the respective economic systems; the laissez-faire economy of Hong Kong versus authoritarian rule in Singapore; loose, indicative planning in Taiwan versus active government control or credit rationing in Korea.[7] Some identify the major source of the NICs' success in various sociological factors, such as the cultural heritage of Confucian ethics. Others cite structural factors, such as equitable land distribution, as crucial explanations for the region's remarkable economic success.[8] Still other writers focus on the international diffusion and borrowing of technologies.[9]

Although many of these explanations are not mutually exclusive, practically all recognize the important contributions of export expansion to the observed development success.

As argued by I.M.D. Little,

the major reasons [for their success] is their labor-intensive export-oriented policies. . . .
Nothing else can account for it. Taiwan and Korea do not have very good capital markets.
Their tax systems are not very good. . . . Planning . . . has not played a key role. More-
over, the nonhuman resources of Taiwan and Korea are not notably favorable to high
income or growth. . . . Luck has played little part in their development. Aid was . . . not
important during the high growth period. Borrowing has remained very important for
Korea but not for the others. Private foreign investment has played a major role in
Singapore; though elsewhere it has played a useful but only minor role.[10]

Therefore, one might conclude that exports matter for growth, though not only
exports. While much of the economic literature attempts to identify and evaluate the
underlying contributive forces fueling the economic performance of the NICs,[11]
very little work has focused on the critical issue of the sources and concomitants of
their export growth. Thus in this book we hope to make a significant contribution to
the understanding of the miracle of the NICs by rigorously examining their rapid
export expansion in the past quarter century.

SIGNIFICANCE OF THE EAST ASIAN DEVELOPMENT MODEL

By the end of the 1980s the four Asian NICs accounted for more than 50% of total
manufactured exports from all developing countries while their population totaled
less than 3% of the population of developing countries.[12] Indeed, very few developing countries have succeeded in expanding their exports to the industrialized countries as the Asian NICs have; other less-developed countries (LDCs), such as the
members of the Organization of Petroleum Exporting Countries (OPEC), have also
"succeeded" in this way, but their experience clearly cannot be duplicated by the
world's developing countries. On the other hand, the success story of the Asian
NICs has generated much enthusiasm in many developing countries seeking opera-
tional benchmarks to map out their development strategies.

In fact, the achievement of the East Asian NICs has aroused much theoretical
debate over whether their development experience—that is, the export-led growth
strategy—can be generalized and adopted as a model for development by other
developing countries.[13] Whether a global universal solution to the world's poverty
problem can be achieved by replicating the East Asian model of development
remains moot, but as the debates and controversies rage, a large group of poor
countries—many members of the Association of South East Asian Nations
(ASEAN)—are today consciously following in the footsteps of the NICs.

After more than two decades of steady growth exceeding 5% a year, the ASEAN
countries of Malaysia, Thailand, the Philippines, and Indonesia have increasingly
become recognized as the "next-tier," "near," or "new" NICs. A somewhat less
scholastic yet generally more popular label for the East Asia NICs is the four "little
tigers," "little dragons," or the "Gang of Four," whereas the ASEAN four are often
designated as the "baby tigers." Implicitly or explicitly, the big tiger is Japan with
its dominant position in world trade and the dominant role model it presents as the
East Asian success story of the post–World War II era.

Given this phenomenal development in East and Southeast Asia, an unmistakable momentum of Pacific dynamism has already altered the international division of labor and the structure of world trade. Since the mid-1980s, two-way trade between the United States and Pacific Basin countries has exceeded the traditional trans-Atlantic trade flows. The U.S. economy has become increasingly integrated with those in the Pacific Basin countries. S. B. Linder argued that if the current trend of relatively faster growth continues for another decade, then the twenty-first century would become a Pacific century. In addition to placing the growth momentum of the East Asian NICs into a global context, Linder further reiterated the role of foreign trade in East Asian development. He concluded that no observer of the NICs could possibly doubt the critical role played by the rapid growth of exports, that is, the adoption of export-oriented strategies to sustain the steady state of growth between 1965 and 1985.[14]

ANATOMY OF SUCCESS

The study of the NICs' export success is crucial for a clear understanding of the mechanisms and strategies that proved so useful and successful in generating the "miracle" of the NICs. In fact, the opening up of economies to international trade and investment is one of four top priorities for action in developing countries set by the World Bank (the other three are investment in human capital, improvement in the climate for enterprise, and institution of appropriate macroeconomic policy).[15] By analyzing the NICs' success in export, we hope to offer important transferable lessons for many other LDCs in their struggle for development. In this regard, this book does not merely report case studies of the unique successes of the four little tigers. The studies undertaken carry important lessons in the general area of trade and development. We of course recognize that nurturance of human capital, governmental support for infrastructures, liberalization of financial institutions, and basic macroeconomic stability are of great importance to economic development. However, in our judgment, the export drive of the NICs co`titutes the major feature and causal factor explaining why the NICs succeeded in breaking their particular vicious circles of poverty in such a short time.[16] Therefore, this book focuses on the sources of trade growth in the NICs and the relationship between the growth of trade and their concurrent and subsequent economic growth.

In devoting this book to an investigation of the export success of the NICs, we analyze the export growth of the NICs in a global context. This context is introduced by a comparison of their export structures with Japan's in an intertemporal, dynamic context. A set of statistical analyses based on the revealed comparative advantages (RCA) and export similarity indices is conducted to evaluate whether they were chasing after Japan and if so, how. To identify the source of their export success— the choice of the right industries (i.e., those enjoying rapidly growing world demand) or the right market destination (focusing on nonstagnant world markets)— we apply constant market share (CMS) analysis.

We go on to analyze whether the next tier of NICs—the ASEAN—are following the ladder of dynamic comparative advantage in the world economy. The likelihood that these ASEAN countries will become tomorrow's NICs is an interesting question in trade and development. We critically evaluate the trade structures in both groups of countries and compare their respective potentials to become tomorrow's NICs.

Common characteristics tend to dominate perceptions of the NICs as a homogeneous group. In fact, intragroup differences between the NICs are often as evident as intergroup differences between the NICs and other developing countries. To analyze particularly the difference in demand responses to the manufactured exports from the NICs, we conducted a series of empirical tests to determine the comparative homogeneity of their exports in the U.S. market.

Since the early 1950s, trade pessimism has dominated the trade policies in the developing countries. It is a fact that exports of primary commodities have long suffered from low income and price elasticities of demand. Moreover, trade liberalization under the auspices of the General Agreement on Tariffs and Trade (GATT) did tend to favor exports of the industrialized countries. Hence the assertion that the GATT is a "rich man's club" is generally accepted as a realistic assessment in the developing countries. The response of the East Asian NICs to trade protection in the industrialized countries is examined in this book. Our findings strongly suggest that having an export structure highly concentrated in primary commodities facing a cascading protective structure need not be an excuse for export retardation. The NICs handled this problem in two distinct ways. They took full advantage of their comparative advantage and promoted low-cost manufactures in the face of "discriminatory" protection. At the same time, they began diversifying their exports to some less sensitive items (more technology-intensive product lines) to avoid trade protectionism. The theoretical underpinnings of the NICs' success are examined in detail; the theory of comparative advantage, the Linder hypothesis, the product cycle theory, and the stage theory of product development are carefully evaluated through empirical tests. The interrelationships between exports and imports are examined in the context of trade flows between the NICs and OECD. Some critical imported materials are identified for the export drive, followed by econometric studies on the intra-industry trade. Finally, a projection of the NICs' exports to the year 2000 is offered.

ORGANIZATION OF THIS BOOK

Following this introductory chapter, chapter 2 examines the dynamic comparative advantage in the NICs.

Chapter 3 traces the sources of the NICs' export growth to evaluate their success with respect to product and market choices. A CMS analysis is utilized to evaluate the sources of export growth by differentiating the market effect, the commodity composition effect, and the competitiveness effect. This analysis enables us to separate the effects of external market environmental forces from internal factors, leading to changes in international competitiveness.

Chapter 4 critically examines the similarities and differences in export patterns among the NICs, comparing them with those of Japan at various historic periods.

By using the similarity index to examine the overlapping of export commodities between the NICs and Japan, relative leaders and laggers in world trade are identified.

Chapter 5 tests the relevance of trade theories to the observed export performances of the NICs. A penetrating examination of underlying product characteristics is used to deduce relevant theoretical arguments regarding their exports.

Chapter 6 is devoted to the problem of reacting to the trade protectionism in the OECD countries. We examine the hypothesis that the NICs tended to consistently and skillfully shift their exports toward those that are less subject to trade barriers.

Chapter 7 focuses on two-way trade between the NICs and the OECD countries. The NICs' drive for export has generated a "boomerang effect," creating increasingly lucrative markets for OECD exporters. Utilizing a Hirschmanian "linkage" model, we analyze the export–import relationship and identify a list of imported products which underpinned the export drive.

Chapter 8 deals with the issue of the comparative homogeneity of the NICs' manufactured exports. Many of the misconceptions in this area arise from the perception that the NICs are all exporting similar products, surging forth in a (collusively?) coordinated drive to "overwhelm" world markets. This hypothesis is explored in this chapter.

Chapter 9 analyzes patterns of inter-industry trade and intra-industry specialization utilizing both parametric and nonparametric econometric tests. Certain cyclical patterns hitherto unnoticed in the literature are observed and commented upon, and several hypotheses consistent with the findings are discussed.

Chapter 10 analyzes the prospects of the next tier of NICs—notably the ASEAN countries. A general concern among development economists is whether there will be another group of "baby tigers," the next tier of NICs in the world economy. Using various aspects of the trade performance of Korea and Taiwan as benchmarks, we survey the records of trade growth in the ASEAN countries.

Chapter 11 examines specific product prospects for future NIC export growth and presents specific product projections to the year 2000.

SUMMARY

The economic systems examined in this book are not merely case studies reflecting the unique success stories of the four little tigers. They carry important lessons in the general area of trade and development. Some of the major findings follow.

The export drive of the NICs constitutes the major feature and causal factor explaining how they succeeded in breaking their particular vicious circles of poverty in such a short period of time.

One major explanation for their success is that the NICs managed both to emulate Japan and to complement rather than directly compete with that country in the OECD markets. By the early 1990s, we find that over 50% of the NIC exports "overlapped" with those of Japan—a finding with significant implications for a consideration of full participation of these countries in institutions such as the OECD and GATT.

The NICs' success in expanding world trade market shares was found to be consistent with the conventional wisdom of expanding trade mainly through exploiting comparative advantage in labor-intensive products in the early period. However, as the last quarter of the twentieth century draws to a close, the picture becomes much more complicated. By the 1970s and later, their comparative advantage gradually shifted to more technology-intensive products. At this point more sophisticated "new" theories of comparative advantage were found to be necessary to fully explain the evolving patterns of competitiveness.

Trade liberalization under the auspices of the GATT has tended to favor the industrialized countries, leading to a consensus that the GATT is a "rich man's club." We uncover some rather surprising insights concerning the relationships between tariff discrimination and the changes in NIC export product mixture over time.

We find that all four NICs' exports were relatively dependent on their imports, especially in the early period. We argue that this is of great interest for "near-NIC" trade policy planning.

Despite their similarities in the general nature of their respective export drives, the NICs differed greatly from one another in many ways. A study of their comparative homogeneity concludes that their drive on exports of high-tech products was highly coordinated in the U.S. market. But this phenomenon was found not to be the case in the traditional labor-intensive products (see chapter 8).

By subdividing the manufactures into research and development (R&D)–intensive versus traditional labor-intensive products, we found that it appeared that the "coordinated surge" was perhaps descriptive of certain relatively small but growing product groups but certainly not of the relatively large, traditional, export products of the NICs.

The proportion of intra-industry, or "two-way," trade was found to be a relatively fast-growing portion of all NIC trade during the period. This is an interesting confirmation of recent findings that the growing dominance of intra-industry trade is not solely a characteristic of industrialized OECD countries in world trade. An examination of underlying determinants of the growing NIC inter-industry trade further supports the proposition that these countries are converging to OECD norms in this area. The identification of temporal consistencies in specialization and diversification patterns suggests the applicability of certain theoretical approaches to explain the successful economic development of these countries.

A careful comparison of trade patterns of ASEAN countries with those relevant to the NICs leads to the conclusion that some of former group, in particular Thailand and Malaysia, are more likely than others (e.g., Indonesia and the Philippines) as candidate "next-tier NICs" in the coming decade.

We find that the macroeconomic structures of the NICs are favorably positioned for an optimistic prognosis concerning the near to midterm future. This is less true in the case of the world trade environment. The process of liberalization, the privatization of public enterprises, the deregulation of financial markets and institutions, and the surge of outbound investment flows are very conducive to further export expansions. In the overall assessment of the NICs to the year 2000, we find that, unless adversely affected by exogenous shocks, the projected trade and implicit industrial structures of Taiwan and Korea may well justify full membership in the OECD and adherence to GATT.

NOTES

1. Kruger (1984):405.
2. The relationship between trade and growth is of course neither simple nor one-sided. As emphasized to us by Ramon Myers, while it is true that the rapid growth of industrial exports allowed for a large-scale restructuring of the NIC economies, this very export growth could not have proceeded without simultaneous high rates of investment and of increases in the capital stock per employee in these countries—much of which required and was supplied by large-scale and growing U.S. industrial exports to these countries.
3. See Chow (1987).
4. For a comprehensive survey of the literature, see Hicks (1990). A good summary on trade and development in the East Asian NICs is also reported in Bradford and Branson (1987).
5. See Ho (1978); Myers and Peattie (1984); and Mason et al. (1979).
6. See Rosenstein-Rodan (1961).
7. See Johnson (1985).
8. See, e.g., Amsden (1991).
9. The various "flying geese" explanations, originally presented by Akamatsu (1962), are of this genre.
10. Little (1981):43.
11. See Hicks (1990) for various interpretations of the success among the NICs.
12. World Bank, *World Development Report, 1991*, p. 10.
13. See, e.g., Cline (1982) and Ranis (1987).
14. Linder (1986).
15. See World Bank, *World Development Report, 1991*, pp. 10–11.
16. It should be noted that A. Lewis's classic thesis concerning the population–trapped dual economies referred specifically to such cases as Taiwan, which in the 1950s appeared hopeless to mainstream development economists.

REFERENCES

Akamatsu, K. 1962. "A Historical Pattern of Economic Growth in Developing Countries." *Developing Economies* no. 1 (March–August):12–21.

Amsden, A. 1991. "Diffusion of Development: The Late Industrializing Model and Greater East Asia." *American Economic Review:* 282–91.

Balassa, Bela. 1981. *The Newly Industrializing Countries in the World Economy*. New York: Pergamon Press.

Bradford, C., and W. Branson (eds.). 1987, *Trade and Structural Change in Pacific Asia*. Chicago: University of Chicago Press.

Cline, William. 1982. "Can the East Asia Model of Development Be Generalized?" *World Development* 10, no. 2:81–90.

Chow, Peter C. Y. 1987. "Causality Between Export Growth and Industrial Development: Empirical Evidence from the NICs." *Journal of Development Economics* 26:55–63.

Hicks, George. 1990. "Explaining the Success of the Four Little Dragons: A Survey." In Seiji Naya and Akira Takayama (eds.), *Economic Development in East and Southeast Asia*. Honolulu: Resource Systems Institute, East–West Center; and Singapore: ASEAN Economic Research Unit, Institute of Southeast Asian Studies, pp. 20–37.

Ho, Samuel P. S. 1978. *Economic Development of Taiwan, 1860–1970*. New Haven: Yale University Press, chapter 3.

Jacoby, Neil H. 1966. *U.S. Aid to Taiwan.* New York: Praeger.

Johnson, Chalmers. 1985. "Political Institutions and Economic Performance: The Government–Business Relationship in Japan, South Korea, and Taiwan." In Robert Scalapino et al. (eds.), *Asian Economic Development: Present and Future.* Berkeley: Institute of East Asian Studies, University of California, pp. 63–89.

Krueger, Anne O. 1984. "Problems of Liberalization." In Arnold Harberger (ed.), *World Economic Growth.* San Francisco: Institute for Contemporary Studies, pp. 403–26.

Linder, Staffan B. 1986. *The Pacific Century: Economic and Political Consequences of Asian–Pacific Dynamism.* Stanford, Calif.: Stanford University Press, pp. 39–48.

Little, I.M.D. 1981. "The Experience and Causes of Rapid Labour-Intensive Development in Korea, Taiwan Province, Hong Kong and Singapore and the Possibility of Emulation." In A. K. Kahn (ed.), *Export-Led Industrialization and Development.* Geneva: International Labor Organization, pp. 23–45.

Mason, Edward S. et al. 1979. *The Economic and Social Modernization of the Republic of Korea.* Cambridge, Mass.: Harvard University Press.

Myers, Ramon H. 1984. "The Economic Transformation of the Republic of China on Taiwan." *China Quarterly* 99:540–52.

Myers, Ramon H., and Mark R. Peattie (eds.). 1984. *The Japanese Colonial Empire, 1895–1945.* Princeton, N.J.: Princeton University Press, chaps. 5–11.

Ranis, Gustav. 1987. "Can the East Asia Model of Development Be Generalized? A Comment." *World Development* 13, no. 4:543–45.

Rosenstein-Rodan, Paul N. 1961. "International Aid for Underdeveloped Countries." *Review of Economics and Statistics* 43, no. 2:107–38.

World Bank. *World Development Report.* Published annually by Oxford University Press.

2

The Comparative Advantage of the NICS

This chapter explicitly examines the "revealed comparative advantage" (RCA) of the NICs over the past two and a half decades. The structural transformation of the merchandise trade in the NICs between 1965 and 1990, and the trend of their continuously increasing market penetration of world manufactured export markets, signaled a possible shift of comparative advantage for the NICs. Following Balassa's thesis of "stages of comparative advantage," the NICs seemed to have taken over certain major product lines from the industrialized countries such as Japan in world trade. It is now expected that the comparative advantages in traditional labor-intensive product lines will gradually shift from the NICs to the next tier of NICs while the NICs expand their exports in relatively technologically intensive product groups.

In fact, economists (e.g., Hadley, Kellman and Landau) have long argued that the process of shifting labor-intensive products away from OECD (and in particular Japan) to the NICs has been clearly under way since the 1960s. However, with the rising wage rates in those NICs in the second half of the 1970s and the early 1980s, their comparative advantages in traditional labor-intensive products is believed by many to be shifting away to the "near-NICs." This concern is reinforced by the increasing momentum of labor movement and environmental protection measures in the NICs, notably in Taiwan and Korea.[1] This plausible phenomenon has provided empirical researchers with a fascinating laboratory for examining the changing pattern, if any, of the comparative advantage in manufactured exports of the Asian NICs.

METHODOLOGY AND QUALIFICATIONS REGARDING THE REVEALED COMPARATIVE ADVANTAGE

In a recent article by Lutz, the shifts of comparative advantage were measured by changes in the export shares in the three-digit product categories of the Standard International Trade Classification (Rev 1) (SITC) 8 (miscellaneous manufactures) and SITC 65 (textiles) with a total number of 25 products. The more comprehensive study reported here extends the product categories to all manufactures at the three-digit SITC level. In this chapter we adopt Balassa's measure of RCA to describe their relative trade performances and competitive abilities.[2]

The index of RCA in each product category is formulated in the following way:

$$RCA_{ij} = \frac{X_{ij}/C_j}{X_i/W}$$

where W = total OECD manufactured imports
            C_j = total OECD imports of the jth product
            X_i = total OECD imports from the ith country
            X_{ij} = OECD imports of the jth product from the ith country.

The numerator in this equation is the percentage share of NICs' exports of the jth product in total imports of that product in the ith country; the denominator is the percentage of NICs' exports in the total imports. Essentially, if a country has comparative advantage in exporting a certain product A to any importing country, then its market share of product A in the importing country will be greater than its share of all imports in the importing country. In this case the RCA index will be greater than 1. Otherwise, it will be less than 1.

There are several qualifications for using the RCA indices to measure the competitiveness of exports among nations. First, the degree of product aggregation may affect the numerical values of the RCA indices. For example, the RCA indices from disaggregated trade data such as five or six digits of SITC product classification would be substantially different from more aggregated data such as one- or two-digit product classifications. Moreover, RCA cannot be used to indicate product differentiation within similar product groups. Grossman found that imports from developed countries tend to be "upmarket" goods, but the same product groups supplied by developing countries are "downmarket" products. For example, exports of Korean Hyundais and Japanese Toyotas are classified as the same product group by SITC category, yet they are aimed at two different segmented markets in the importing countries.

Finally, the importing country could apply discriminatory trade policies to different exporters. Hence existing preferential treatments could deny trade competitors equal access to the importing market. Nevertheless, given these qualifications, the RCA indices can still provide us with important information about the relative trade performances of the NICS.

The product classification used in this book is the three-digit SITC product category (Rev 1), which covers more than 100 manufactured products, and conceptually includes all manufactured trade. Those manufactured products accounted for more than 90% of total exports in the Asian NICs in the late 1980s. Unless elsewhere specified, all the trade data used in this book were obtained from Data Resources Incorporated/McGraw-Hill and are based on OECD Series C (Detailed Trade by Commodity). Whereas the analyses performed were calculated at this (more-than-100-product) level of disaggregation, the tabular presentations are given for a more highly aggregated grouping of 13 product groups.[3]

DEVELOPMENT OF THE REVEALED COMPARATIVE ADVANTAGE IN THE OECD MARKET

Tables 2.1 through 2.4 indicate the RCA indices of each NIC in the OECD market for selected years from 1965 to 1990. To better understand the results summarized in the tables, it is important to realize that an exporting country is said to have a revealed comparative advantage in a product whenever its RCA index is greater than unity. Such an index indicates that the exports of the NIC are more highly concentrated in that product than are the imports of the OECD.

Table 2.5 ranks, in descending order, those products in which each of the NICs enjoyed a comparative advantage in 1965 and in 1990. In 1965 all four NICs were found to enjoy a comparative advantage only in textiles and clothing. In 1990 the only product group in which all four shared a comparative advantage was electrical machinery. Of the four NICs, Singapore experienced the most radical change in the pattern of its comparative advantage. It was the only NIC that experienced no overlap whatsoever. That is, of the product groups in which it enjoyed a comparative advantage in 1990, not one of them was on the comparable list in 1966.

It is evident that in the early period, the revealed comparative advantage of the Asian NICs lay in those product groups which are generally classified as traditional labor-intensive products. Among them, textiles, clothing, footwear, and furniture are the four major product groups in which the NICs had enjoyed their comparative advantage as they adopted their export-led growth strategies in the mid-1960s. However, their competitive positions have changed since the 1970s. The most significant phenomenon is the steady decline of their competitiveness in textile products after the United States and certain European countries adopted more innovative, capital-intensive methods to manufacture textile products in the OECD countries. The second reason for this relative decline is trade barriers such as the Multifiber Agreement (MFA), which limited annual imports of textile products from the NICs. The third and probably most important reason is the increasing relative

Table 2.1 Revealed Comparative Advantage of Hong Kong in OECD

Product Group	1965	1970	1975	1980	1985	1990
Chemicals	0.02	0.04	0.03	0.02	0.04	0.06
Metal manufactures	0.14	0.19	0.21	0.26	0.29	0.30
Nonferrous metals	0.02	0.02	0.06	0.12	0.04	0.04
Textiles	1.71	1.29	1.09	0.73	0.62	0.65
Nonelectrical machinery	0.02	0.10	0.18	0.33	0.53	0.50
Electrical machinery	0.97	1.37	1.28	1.25	1.21	1.18
Transport equipment	0.07	0.04	0.02	0.02	0.02	0.02
Precision instruments	0.41	0.40	0.50	0.70	0.75	1.05
Clothing	11.64	9.39	9.69	8.03	7.59	6.94
Furniture	1.24	0.62	0.60	0.52	0.30	0.20
Footwear	3.52	2.30	0.83	0.73	0.72	0.57
Resource-based products	0.32	0.26	0.31	0.33	0.32	0.43
Miscellaneous manufactures	4.02	4.80	2.98	3.92	3.01	2.75

Table 2.2 Revealed Comparative Advantage of Korea in OECD

Product Group	1965	1970	1975	1980	1985	1990
Chemicals	0.13	0.10	0.15	0.26	0.18	0.25
Metal manufactures	0.18	0.24	0.69	1.48	1.69	1.35
Nonferrous metals	0.33	0.10	0.04	0.10	0.06	0.09
Textiles	3.14	2.45	2.15	1.80	1.37	1.13
Nonelectrical machinery	0.06	0.02	0.10	0.11	0.30	0.53
Electrical machinery	0.17	0.86	1.44	1.52	1.64	1.67
Transport equipment	0.02	0.00	0.02	0.03	0.07	0.28
Precision instruments	0.02	0.14	0.38	0.41	0.39	0.39
Clothing	6.34	7.42	6.39	5.62	4.66	3.47
Furniture	0.06	0.05	0.24	0.28	0.34	0.40
Footwear	7.55	2.27	4.35	5.89	5.63	6.63
Resource-based products	2.18	1.83	0.88	0.72	0.57	0.44
Miscellaneous manufactures	1.21	3.36	2.08	1.59	1.71	1.60

Table 2.3 Revealed Comparative Advantage of Taiwan in OECD

Product Group	1965	1970	1975	1980	1985	1990
Chemicals	1.06	0.17	0.13	0.17	0.14	0.19
Metal manufactures	0.15	0.28	0.40	0.69	1.01	1.16
Nonferrous metals	0.14	0.04	0.02	0.02	0.07	0.15
Textiles	1.80	1.46	1.22	0.83	0.78	0.88
Nonelectrical machinery	0.01	0.12	0.21	0.33	0.67	1.14
Electrical machinery	0.95	2.76	2.20	2.03	1.61	1.57
Transport equipment	0.03	0.07	0.08	0.13	0.17	0.27
Precision instruments	0.08	0.21	0.46	0.58	0.67	0.75
Clothing	5.34	7.17	5.21	3.54	2.63	1.58
Furniture	1.60	1.67	1.36	2.37	3.50	2.73
Footwear	2.55	5.57	6.72	7.23	6.12	3.61
Resource-based products	2.31	1.12	0.75	0.83	0.73	0.58
Miscellaneous manufactures	1.63	1.71	2.30	2.64	2.22	2.05

Table 2.4 Revealed Comparative Advantage of Singapore in OECD

Product Group	1965	1970	1975	1980	1985	1990
Chemicals	1.42	0.12	0.37	0.26	0.43	0.52
Metal manufactures	1.44	0.02	0.10	0.12	0.21	0.16
Nonferrous metals	0.73	0.07	0.05	0.15	0.17	0.09
Textiles	0.90	0.74	0.27	0.32	0.07	0.07
Nonelectrical machinery	0.45	0.15	0.75	0.56	1.90	2.51
Electrical machinery	0.82	5.80	5.12	5.92	3.61	2.67
Transport equipment	0.53	0.15	0.07	0.21	0.17	0.05
Precision instruments	0.56	0.08	3.62	1.28	0.73	0.50
Clothing	0.56	3.76	1.92	1.88	1.40	0.95
Furniture	1.52	0.06	0.43	0.95	0.88	0.47
Footwear	1.08	0.47	0.05	0.13	0.02	0.05
Resource-based products	1.27	1.28	0.60	0.34	0.18	0.17
Miscellaneous manufactures	1.94	1.58	1.18	1.06	0.71	0.85

Table 2.5 Demonstrated Comparative Advantage, Selected Product Groups, 1965 and 1990

Product Group	Taiwan		Korea		Singapore		Hong Kong	
	1965	1990	1965	1990	1966	1990	1965	1990
Textiles	X	N	X	X	X	N	X	N
Clothing	X	X	X	X	X	N	X	X
Footwear	X	X	X	X	N	N	X	N
Furniture	X	X	N	N	N	N	X	N
Resource-based products	X	N	X	N	X	N	N	N
Miscellaneous manufactures	X	X	X	X	N	N	X	X
Chemicals	X	N	N	N	N	N	N	N
Metal manufactures	N	X	N	X	N	N	N	N
Nonelectrical machinery	N	X	N	N	N	X	N	N
Electrical machinery	N	X	N	X	N	X	N	X

Henceforth Singapore's earliest year will be 1966 rather than 1965 (due to a large number of missing values for the earlier year).
Note: X indicates the presence of revealed comparative advantages, N its absence.

labor costs in the Asian NICs. As a result, the relative competitiveness of textile products declined substantially after the mid-1970s.

Among the most significant shifts of comparative advantage in the NICs were trends in exports of electrical machinery and resource-based products. Aside from Hong Kong, comparative advantage in resource-based products characterized the NICs in the mid-1960s, but by 1990 this was true of none of them. Conversely, in the earlier period not one of the NICs demonstrated a comparative advantage in electrical machinery, a situation that was completely reversed by the early 1990s.

One may generalize that all the NICs in East Asia have successfully upgraded their exports from labor-intensive and resource-based products to more technology-intensive products in the period after the 1970s.

THE DYNAMICS OF CHANGING COMPARATIVE ADVANTAGE IN THE NIC–OECD MARKET

As was noted earlier, the RCA indices were used as an indicator of the relative trade performances for the NICs. If the relative competitive position of a nation's exports had indeed undergone substantial dynamic changes, then the RCA indices between two time periods would tend to be less significantly correlated with one another. In order to evaluate the degree of changing comparative advantage in the NICs during the period under investigation, we compare the Spearman rank correlation coefficients between each country's own RCA indices in 1990 and its RCA indices in the previous years. As noted earlier, all 101 three-digit SITC products, rather than the 13 product groups, are used to calculate the RCA indices of each country in every time period. Results are reported in Table 2.6.

From Table 2.6, one may note that Singapore experienced the most profound structural changes in its pattern of comparative advantage. The relative rankings of Singapore's RCA indices in 1990 not only are not significantly positively correlated

Table 2.6   Spearman Rank Correlation Coefficients
Between RCA Indices for 1990 and the Specific Year
Indices for the NICs in OECD ($N = 101$)

	Korea	Hong Kong	Singapore	Taiwan
1965	0.24[a]	0.77[a]	−0.17	0.49[b]
1970	0.49[b]	0.79[b]	0.40[b]	0.74[b]
1975	0.70[b]	0.85[b]	0.60[b]	0.79[b]
1980	0.76[b]	0.91[b]	0.73[b]	0.90[b]
1985	0.88[b]	0.92[b]	0.88[b]	0.93[b]

N = number of observations.
[a]Significant at the 95% level.
[b]Significant at the 99% level.

but indeed are negatively correlated with its 1965 RCA.[4] This implies that the competitive position of Singaporean exports in 1990 was substantially different form what it was in 1965. Referring earlier to Tables 2.4 and 2.5, we noted that Singapore's comparative advantage in 1990 mostly lay in electrical and non-electrical machinery (i.e., RCAs of 2.67 and 2.51, respectively) whereas in 1965 the RCA indices in those two product groups were less than 1. The products in which Singapore had strong RCA (i.e., RCA greater than 1 in 1965)—chemicals, textiles, furniture, and resource-based products—declined substantially in international competitiveness, as reflected in their RCA indices in 1990.

The country that experienced the second most radical structural transformation in export competitiveness is Korea. The ranking of Korean RCA indices in 1990 was only 0.24, significantly similar to (correlated with) the respective 1965 values (not significant at the 1% level). During the period between 1965 and 1990, Korea had gained substantial export competitiveness in electrical machinery and metal manufactures. The RCA indices of these two product groups were less than 1 in 1965, yet they jumped to one of the highest by 1990.

Relatively speaking, the structural change in the pattern of comparative advantage was notably slower in Taiwan than in Korea. Taiwan's 1965 pattern of revealed comparative advantage was twice as highly correlated with its respective 1990 pattern than was the case for Korea. Furthermore, Korea's rapid structural transformation in its dynamic pattern of comparative advantage continued to outpace Taiwan's during the latter half of the 1980s, as judged by the respective correlation coefficients between the 1985 and 1990 RCA values. One explanation for the relative failure of Taiwan's RCA pattern to shift over time (relative to Singapore and Korea, but not relative to Hong Kong!) is that more than 90% of Taiwanese enterprises are characterized as "small and medium business," which a priori would be expected to be less responsive and more conservative than the large-scale enterprises characteristic of the Korean manufacturing structure. This explanation suggests that in an environment calling for bold, relatively major shifts in production and export patterns along with rapid economic growth, government-supported "industrial policy" may not necessarily be dominated by a free market, laissez-faire policy. This hypothesis is given additional credence by the experience of Singapore, which underwent the most significant shift in its export competitiveness pattern over the full 25-year period. In Singapore, the government deliberately promoted technology-intensive industries in the 1970s using measures that included mandatory increases of its labor costs. Hence government policy under the authoritarian rule in Singapore could push toward structural transformation much faster than Taiwan. Again, these examples do not prove that authoritarian rule is the right way to implement industrial development policy but merely indicate that consciously directed government policy can prove decisive in pursuing economic development goals. This is a line of thinking worth considering in today's intellectual climate in which, with the collapse of the "ruble bloc," deviations from the laissez-faire mindset at times take on the hue of heresy.

Of course, an alternative hypothesis could be simply that Taiwan's original RCA pattern was closer to the long-run optimum, and hence called for less change. The likelihood that this was the case is explored in chapter 3, utilizing a detailed year-by-year constant market share analysis.

The structural transformation of commodity composition of exports in Hong Kong is the smallest of the Asian NICs. Its 1965 RCA pattern had a relatively high 0.77 rank correlation with its 1990 RCA pattern. In Table 2.5 we note that two of the three product groups in which Hong Kong had a demonstrated comparative advantage 1990 were on the respective list in 1965.

COMPETITIVENESS VERSUS COMPLEMENTARITY IN THE NICS' EXPORTS IN THE OECD MARKET

Ever since the NICs emerged in the world economy two decades ago, they have been exporting large volumes of "similar" products to the OECD markets. An interesting question is whether they are competing with one another at the specific product level. In this section we assess the competitiveness versus complementarity of their exports by conducting some nonparametric tests. In examining the trade relations among the industrialized nations, the NICs, and other developing countries, Lutz used the correlation coefficients of changes in export shares in some selected manufactured products—that is, three-digit categories of SITC 8 (miscellaneous manufactures) and 65 (textiles)—between pairs of countries to determine the probable shifts of comparative advantage between them. If both countries gained their shares of exports on these product groups, Lutz suggested, then the positive correlation would support the argument that "no evidence that shifts in comparative advantage had been occurring but rather that there was a complementary export expansion for country pairs."[5]

To extend Lutz's methodology to evaluate the competitive/complementary status of exports in the NICs, we will conduct a series of nonparametric tests on their RCA indices here. The coverage of our product groups, which include all 101 three-digit SITC products, is much more comprehensive than what Lutz did. Moreover, instead of using a simple market share, we use the index of RCA, which reveals not only the relative market shares of specific products, but also the country's share in the importing country.

If the RCA indices of a pair of countries on the same product group are positively

Table 2.7 Rank Correlation Coefficients Between RCA Indices for Pairs of NICs (time series, 1965–90)

Product Group	Taiwan/Korea	Taiwan/Singapore	Taiwan/Hong Kong	Korea/Singapore	Korea/Hong Kong	Singapore/Hong Kong
Chemicals	-0.25	0.03	-0.32	0.38[b]	0.10	0.24
Resource-based products	0.91[c]	0.90[c]	0.10	0.97[c]	0.01	0.04
Metal manufactures	0.85[c]	0.58	0.94[c]	0.53[c]	0.82[c]	0.54[c]
Nonferrous metals	0.42[b]	0.09	-0.06	0.47[b]	-0.04	0.27
Textiles	0.87[c]	0.79[c]	0.94[c]	0.86[c]	0.93[c]	0.88[c]
Nonelectrical machinery	0.91[c]	0.79[c]	0.95[c]	0.89[c]	0.86[c]	0.74[c]
Electrical machinery	-0.52[c]	0.31	0.65[c]	0.10	-0.34[a]	0.09
Transport equipment	0.89[c]	-0.36[a]	-0.53[c]	-0.39[b]	-0.57[c]	0.25
Precision instruments	0.63[c]	0.07	0.86[c]	0.46[b]	0.65[c]	-0.07
Clothing	0.96[c]	0.81[c]	0.92[c]	0.77[c]	0.85[c]	0.73[c]
Furniture	0.45[b]	0.60[c]	-0.69[c]	0.34[b]	-0.38[a]	-0.30
Footwear	0.01	-0.15	-0.20	-0.45[b]	-0.35[a]	0.66[c]
Miscellaneous manufactures	-0.28	0.07	-0.31	0.19	0.35[a]	0.41[b]

[a]Significant at the 90% level.
[b]Significant at the 95% level.
[c]Significant at the 99% level.

correlated over a period of time, then one would conclude that the competitive edges of exports in these two countries have been moving in the same direction. Hence the status of their export competitiveness is complementary. On the other hand, if they are negatively correlated, then the country with increasing comparative advantage would tend to replace the other, which has a declining RCA index on the same product group. In this case, one may conclude that these two countries are in a competitive status. Results from the nonparametric tests are reported on Table 2.7.

The results from Table 2.7 suggest that one cannot generalize concerning the competitiveness or complementarity over time of the inter-NIC export compositions. In some product categories—notably textiles, clothing (effects of the MFA?), and nonelectrical machinery—high positive correlations indicate that over time the competitiveness patterns of all four NICs moved more or less in tandem. On the other hand, there are many products in which significant negative correlations signify competitive replacement. This is noted for the cases of electrical machinery (Taiwan/Korea, Hong Kong/Korea) and transport equipment (Taiwan/Singapore, Taiwan/Hong Kong, Korea/Singapore, and Korea/Hong Kong). Similar competitive replacement was indicated for one more traditional product, furniture (Taiwan/Hong Kong). Finally, there are many products for which no statistically significant correlation between RCA time trends were indicated between the various NIC pairs.

Thus it is hard to generalize from the results summarized in Table 2.7. In chapter 8 we apply a statistical test to examine the proposition that NIC export patterns generally are complementary.

SUMMARY

The structure of export commodities among the NICs has substantially shifted away from traditional labor-intensive products to more technology-intensive ones. With the exception of Singapore, they still have a relative production (and specialization) bias in favor of traditional labor-intensive product groups, such as clothing. However, the extent of this relative concentration is demonstrably far less than it had been in earlier periods. For many labor-intensive products, the NICs have in fact lost their revealed comparative advantage. In other words, their own relative degree of production concentration in these products is lower than the relative concentration in imports of their OECD markets. Furthermore, the NICs have clearly gained comparative advantage in relatively high-technology products.

It was found that the speed of dynamic shifts in comparative advantage is far from homogeneous across NICs. Singapore seems to be the front runner in terms of the speed of industrialization, followed by Korea and Taiwan. Hong Kong seems to be slowest in shifting export structure. Even though the NICs have been exporting roughly similar product groups in the OECD market, most of their export expansions are complementary rather than mutually competitive. Competition appears in only a few cases, such as transport equipment and furniture, under which both Korea and Taiwan had significant negative correlation coefficients with Hong Kong, and footwear, in which both Korea and Taiwan demonstrated a limited degree of negative correlation coefficients with Hong Kong and Singapore. With these few exceptions, there is no significant evidence that exports from the four little tigers have been replacing one another in the same market segments.

Appendix Table 2.1 Classification of 13 Product Groups by Three-Digit SITC

Product Group	SITC
Chemicals	512–15, 521, 531–33, 541, 551, 553–54, 561, 571, 581, 599
Metal manufactures	671–79, 691–98
Nonferrous metals	681–89
Textiles	651–57
Nonelectrical machinery	711–12, 714–19
Electrical machinery	722–19
Transport equipment	731–35
Precision instruments	861
Clothing	841–42
Furniture	821
Footwear	851
Resource-based products	611–13, 621, 629, 631–33, 641–42, 661–67
Miscellaneous products	812, 831, 862, 863, 864, 891–99

NOTES

1. Both of these social movements would adversely affect the international competitiveness of the labor-intensive products in Taiwan and Korea. In fact, there were indications that the shortage of unskilled labor in Taiwan had appeared in the early 1980s.

2. The RCA indices used here reflect the competitiveness of exporting countries as well as the changes on the demand of the importing countries. However, Lee (1980) conducted a decomposition analysis and found that the "competitiveness effect is the overwhelming factor in the change of market share for Korea and Taiwan" (17).

3. The details of the aggregation of these 13 product groups are reported in Appendix Table 2.1.

4. It must, however, be noted that Singapore's trade coverage for 1965 appears spotty. Hence little significance attaches to the negative correlation. In general, we utilize 1966 as the earliest reliable date for Singapore.

5. Lutz (1987):347.

REFERENCES

Balassa, Bela. 1965. "Trade Liberalization and Revealed Comparative Advantage," *Manchester School of Economics and Social Studies* 33:99–123.

———. 1979. "The Changing Pattern of Comparative Advantage in Manufactured Goods." *Review of Economics and Statistics* 61:259–66.

———. 1983. *The Newly Industrializing Countries in the World Economy.* New York: Pergamon Press, pp. 149–67.

Chow, Peter C. Y. 1987. "Causality Between Export Growth and Industrial Development: Empirical Evidence from the NICs." *Journal of Development Economics* 26:55–63.

Grossman, Gene M. 1982. "Import Competition from Developed and Developing Countries." *Review of Economics and Statistics* 14, no. 2:271–81.

Hadley, Eleanor G. 1981. "Japan's Export Competitiveness in Third World Markets." In Center for Strategic and International Studies (ed.), *World Trade Competition and Third World Markets.* New York: Praeger, pp. 252–330.

Haufbauer, G. C., and J. G. Chilas. 1974. "Specialization by Industrial Countries: Extent and Consequences." in H. Giersch (ed.), *The International Division of Labor: Problems and Prospects.* Tübingen: Mohr, pp. 3–38.

Kellman, Mitchell, and D. Laudau. 1984. "The Nature of Japan's Comparative Advantage, 1965–80." *World Development* 12, no. 4:433–38.

Larry, Hal B. 1984. *Imports of Manufactures from Less-Developed Countries.* New York: National Bureau of Economic Research.

Lee, Y. S. 1980. *An Analysis of the Comparative Advantage of Korean Export Commodities.* Seoul: Korean International Economic Institute.

———. 1986. "Changing Export Patterns in Korea, Taiwan and Japan." *Weltwirtschaftiches Archiv* 122, no. 1:150–63.

Lutz, James M. 1987. "Shifting Comparative Advantage, the NICs, and the Developing Countries." *International Trade Journal* 1, no. 4:339–58.

3

The Sources of Export Growth

Between 1965 and 1990 the four East Asian NICs substantially increased their overall shares of world markets. In this chapter we ask the following question: To what extent can these successes and relative successes be ascribed to external (demand) factors compared with internal (supply) factors?

The analytical tool we utilize is the constant market share (CMS) analysis, as developed by Leamer and Stern.[1] Appendix Table 3.1 presents annual sets of constant market share tables for each of the four NICs. For each year, from 1965 to 1990, these identify the percentage by which each country exceeded the world rate of trade growth, or the world trend. As summarized in Table 3.1, the figures indicate that during the past quarter century the four NICs, except Korea and Hong Kong during the last five-year period, steadily increased their market shares in the OECD.[2] The resultant market shares, defined as manufactured imports into OECD markets from a given NIC, divided by total manufactured imports into these markets, are seen in Table 3.2.

The relatively rapid penetration of the OECD import markets—especially the U.S. and Japanese markets—by the NIC manufactures is dramatic. This chapter examines this phenomenon and the possible reasons for these increases in world (OECD) shares over time.

The constant market share technique decomposes the degree by which each NIC's exports exceeded world trade trends into three separate factors: the market effect, the commodity effect, and the competitiveness effect. The market effect measures the extent to which the excess of each NIC's growth rate over overall market growth may be explained in terms of the market-destination pattern; the commodity effect focuses on the patterns of commodity specialization; and the competitiveness effect indicates that part of the export success which is related to neither of the two.

Both the market effect and the commodity effect may be considered external demand factors. The first will register as positive if the particular (OECD) market in which the NIC's exports are relatively concentrated tended to grow relatively faster than the rest of the OECD markets. The second will register as positive if the products in which the NICs are relatively specialized experienced higher than average world demand growth. Since from one year to the next fluctuations in OECD economies and markets tended to occur substantially more rapidly than annual

Table 3.1 Average Annual Percentage by Which NIC
Exports Exceeded World Trade Trends

	Taiwan	Korea	Singapore	Hong Kong
1966–70	39.9	41.1	38.5	3.5
1971–75	29.3	20.7	44.6	1.1
1976–80	9.2	14.3	12.6	6.1
1981–85	8.5	11.7	9.2	3.0
1986–90	4.3	−2.3	9.9	−5.9

Since 1965 data were not available for Singapore, we substitute 1966 data for
that country throughout this chapter.

changes in NIC export markets, or product compositions, and were clearly not
under the control of the NICs, the market effect and the commodity effect are clearly
"external" factors from the viewpoint of the NIC.[3] Conversely, since the competitiveness effect is independent of changes in overall OECD demand patterns (it
measures changes in market shares within product–market cells), it may be viewed
as an internal (supply-oriented) factor.

We ask first whether the demand-oriented, external commodity and market effects
tended to have a markedly different or similar pattern in the NICs over time. Table
3.3, drawing on Appendix Table 3.1, indicates those years in which each of these
two effects exerted a negative effect on each of the NIC's exports.

Table 3.2 NIC Shares of Manufactured Imports
in Major OECD Markets, 1965–90 (%)

	Taiwan	Korea	Singapore	Hong Kong
U.S. Market				
1965	0.52	0.38	0.07	2.78
1970	1.89	1.38	0.22	3.37
1975	3.29	2.60	0.72	2.82
1980	5.34	3.22	1.24	3.61
1985	6.62	4.01	1.43	3.37
1990	5.84	4.84	2.40	2.43
EC Market				
1965	0.03	0.03	0.03	0.97
1970	0.11	0.06	0.05	0.87
1975	0.44	0.41	0.23	1.05
1980	0.69	0.63	0.32	1.16
1985	0.78	0.66	0.37	1.00
1990	1.14	0.80	0.62	0.97
Japanese Market				
1965	0.19	0.24	0.03	0.84
1970	1.52	1.65	0.05	1.09
1975	3.06	6.86	0.72	1.62
1980	4.10	7.12	0.79	1.38
1985	4.87	7.05	1.06	1.53
1990	5.17	8.38	1.47	1.59

Table 3.3   Years in Which World Demand Factors Aided or Impeded NIC Export Expansion

	Taiwan		Korea		Singapore		Hong Kong	
	Commodity	Market	Commodity	Market	Commodity	Market	Commodity	Market
1966	–		–		NA	NA	–	
1967	–		–		–		–	
1968					–			
1969		–		–		–		–
1970		–	–			–	–	–
1971		–		–				–
1972								
1973		–				–	–	–
1974	–	–	–	–	–	–	–	–
1975		–		–		–		–
1976								
1977		–		–		–		–
1978					–			
1979	–	–	–	–	–	–	–	–
1980	–	–	–	–	–	–	–	–
1981								
1982								
1983	–		–				–	
1984								
1985				–		–	–	
1986		–		–		–		–
1987		–		–		–		–
1988	–	–	–	–			–	–
1989		–	–			–		
1990		–		–		–		–

Note: A dash indicates a negative effect.

From Table 3.3 it appears that the commodity and the market effects were dispersed fairly randomly throughout the period from 1965 to 1990. Furthermore, they did tend to affect each of the four NICs in a fairly similar manner, both in relative frequency and in timing. Each one of the NICs experienced between 7 and 11 years of negative commodity effects and between 11 and 13 of negative market effects. These, in turn, were similarly grouped or clustered. Thus from 1966 to 1967 all NICs experienced negative commodity effects. During the post–OPEC-I period (1973–80), all of them encountered negative market effects in most of these years (during these eight years Korea experienced five such negative effects; all of the others experienced six). In fact, during this period the negative market effects were so strong that even in the face of positive "competitiveness" effects some countries actually lost overall market shares (as evidenced by negative world trend effects in Appendix Table 3.1). This was true for Korea in 1975 and 1979, Taiwan in 1974, and Singapore in 1977. In the following four years (1981–84) all four NICs experienced positive market effects, while the latter part of the last decade—similar to the end of the 1970s—saw typically negative market and commodity effects.

Thus the two demand-related effects, dependent primarily on OECD market developments, tended to affect each of the four NICs in a fairly uniform manner vis-à-vis each other and over time. On the other hand, the internal, supply-related competitiveness effect differed significantly in frequency among the NICs and was concentrated in particular time periods. In frequency of occurrence, of 26 years, negative competitiveness effects were found 12 times in Hong Kong, 5 times in both Taiwan and Korea, and 3 times in Singapore. In both Taiwan and Korea, the preponderance of these negative competitiveness measures—80% for Korea and 90% for Taiwan—occurred in the last 6 years, from 1985 through 1990. Though less concentrated in the last period, a general decrease in internal-related competitive stance is also evident for Hong Kong, where 42% of all negative competitiveness effects occurred during these last 6 years. Singapore, with 30% such occurrences in this latter period, is the only one of the NICs not indicating internal, supply-related "temporal diminishing returns" in international competitiveness.

In this chapter we discuss the growth of market share in three subperiods. The first (1965–73) was a period marked by rapid expansion in world trade. The expanding imports of the OECD afforded great opportunities to those countries that embraced export expansion as a conscious strategy. This was the period of the emergence of the NICs as a recognizable (and successful) economic phenomenon. The second subperiod (1973–82) was a relatively stagnant period beginning with the upheavals and dislocations of the first OPEC energy crisis and ending with those associated with the second. The final period analyzed (1982–87) reflects more recent developments. In each case, we illustrate a typical year utilizing the relevant CMS figures.

THE "TAKE-OFF," 1965–1973

As noted, the mid-1960s marked the beginning of the "take-off" for the NICs, except perhaps for Hong Kong, which may be argued to have taken off earlier. In 1965 the manufactured exports of all four East Asian NICs constituted only 1.7% of all OECD-manufactured imports. Roughly 80% of all NIC-manufactured exports (henceforth "exports") were those of Hong Kong. During the subsequent eight years, world trade expanded at unprecedented rates; the average annual rate was a remarkable 18.9%, as indicated in the second column of Table 3.4.

During this period, the NICs as a group more than doubled their share of the manufactured imports into the OECD (including intra-EC trade), rising from 1.7%

Table 3.4 Average Annual Growth Rates
of World Manufactured Trade (%)

	1965–87	1965–73	1973–82	1982–87
U.S.	16.5	18.9	14.4	16.5
EC	14.3	18.3	11.5	12.9
Japan	17.2	25.8	11.4	14.9
OECD	15.1	18.9	12.3	14.2

in 1965 to 4.1 in 1973. Except for Hong Kong (which grew a bit slower than the world markets), each of the other NICs grew at an average annual rate of close to 50%.

To what extent can this unprecedented (and unrepeated) performance be explained in terms of (possibly prescient, but more likely fortuitous) product and market positioning? Let us begin by examining the initial market-destination positioning of the four NICs in 1966 (Table 3.5). It is clear that South Korea and Taiwan were substantially more dependent on the U.S. market than were Singapore and Hong Kong. Since both the EC and the U.S. import markets grew roughly at the same rate during this period, this particular difference would probably not account for much of a difference in performance. South Korea might have been best positioned since it directed a proportion of its exports at least twice as high as that of the other NICs to the relatively rapidly growing Japanese import market for manufactures. Singapore and Hong Kong may be seen to be least advantageously positioned, since they had the smallest proportion directed to the fastest growing market segment (Japan) and the highest proportion directed to the slowest growing (EC). In terms of the constant market share analysis, South Korea would be found to have the best market effect. Since the relative market growth rates in fact changed from year to year, as did the relative proportions directed to specific markets for each of the NICs, the year-to-year CMS analysis is required for any but the most heuristic and illustrative analysis, such as that just outlined.

Despite South Korea's apparent marketing advantage, Taiwan's exports grew more rapidly during this period, and Singapore's almost as rapidly. Can one ascribe this to (strategic or again fortuitous) product specialization? It may be that a given country will gain market shares because it specializes in products whose world demand is especially growing. To illustrate this effect, summarized as the commodity effect in the CMS analysis, Table 3.6 presents the respective proportions of product specialization in 1966 and the actual world growth rates of each of these products from 1966 to 1967. From the last column of Table 3.6 it is noted that a wide discrepancy existed in the world trade growth rates of the various commodities from 1966 to 1967. These ranged from an increase of 25.8% for transport equipment to a decline of 11% for textiles. From the first four columns of the table we note a wide variation in the NICs' respective patterns of specialization. These two factors provide an a priori likelihood that the commodity effect could prove to be an important factor in explaining the differences between the NICs in their export performance during those years.

An examination of the figures in Table 3.6 suggest that in the mid-1960s all of the NICs were poorly positioned in this regard. Each had a high proportion of its

Table 3.5 Market Distribution of NIC Exports, 1966 (%)

Destination	South Korea	Taiwan	Singapore	Hong Kong
U.S.	80.5	84.5	50.1	48.7
EC	11.1	10.9	47.0	48.2
Japan	8.4	4.6	2.9	3.1

Table 3.6 Distribution of NIC Exports for 1966 and Growth in World Imports by Product Group, 1966–67

Product Group	Percentage of NIC Exports				OECD Import Growth (%)
	Taiwan	South Korea	Singapore	Hong Kong	
Chemicals	7.0	1.5	2.8	3.2	12.7
Metal manufactures	1.7	2.1	0.7	1.9	7.0
Nonferrous metals	1.0	3.5	2.9	0.3	0.7
Textiles	12.9	24.2	14.5	13.1	−11.0
Nonelectrical machinery	0.4	1.0	13.6	0.4	11.9
Electrical machinery	14.5	1.2	2.0	10.5	11.5
Transport equipment	0.2	0.2	5.8	0.6	25.8
Precision instruments	0.1	0.1	0.2	0.9	9.5
Clothing	18.8	19.0	31.4	39.5	6.6
Furniture	1.5	0.1	0.1	0.5	11.7
Footwear	4.4	5.7	0.1	3.4	12.1
Resource-based products	27.4	28.9	24.8	5.2	−0.04
Miscellaneous manufactures	10.1	15.7	1.2	23.6	11.7

exports concentrated in the slow-growing (or even declining) sectors of textiles and clothing. For both sectors, the respective percentages were 43% for Korea, 32% for Taiwan, 53% for Hong Kong, and 46% for Singapore. It is obvious that a country's export performance is not likely to be brilliant when close to half of its exports are concentrated in products whose world export demand is stagnant or even declining. And indeed, all four exhibited a negative commodity effect, as indicated in Table 3.7.

The preceding analysis makes clear that there is one obvious strategy which may be pursued that holds a high likelihood for a successful export drive. A country whose exports are highly concentrated or specialized in product groups that exhibit stagnant or declining world demand could still gain world market shares by competitively displacing others from the markets in which it holds a comparative advantage. This seems to have been the strategy followed by Hong Kong in the 1965–73 period. Comparison of Tables 3.6 and 3.10 shows that the period saw practically no change in the product distribution of Hong Kong's exports. A different strategy, although likely to be costly in the short run, would be to flexibly react to world market trends, switching one's revealed comparative advantage from the (traditional) stagnant product sectors to more rapidly expanding segments. This seems to

Table 3.7 Constant Market Share Analysis, 1967 (annual changes)

Measure	South Korea	Taiwan	Singapore	Hong Kong
Greater than world trend	47.6	40.1	−23.2	3.3
Commodity composition effect	−4.2	−3.1	−4.6	−3.2
Market distribution effect	4.7	1.6	1.0	0.5
Competitiveness effect	47.0	41.6	−19.7	5.9

This CMS table, as well as all of the others in this chapter, are selected from the comprehensive tables in Appendix Table 3.1.

have been the strategy undertaken by Singapore, which had experienced the greatest change in product composition of its exports during this period. To a somewhat lesser extent, Taiwan also appears to have taken this approach in the mid- to late 1960s.

The constant market analysis presented in Table 3.7 does indeed suggest that from 1966 to 1967 the performance of each of the NICs was lowered by roughly 10%, or 3 to 4 percentage points, due to poor commodity positioning with respect to world demand trends. Were this commodity effect absent, South Korea's and Taiwan's exports would have improved by roughly 10%. Hong Kong's would have doubled, from 3.3% better than world trend to 6.5% better.

During the period 1965 to 1973, "bad" years of negative world demand (commodity and market) effects alternated regularly with "good" years of positive effects, thus tending to cancel each other over the entire period. In any case, the internal supply-related competitiveness effects tended to be relatively dominant during this period, explaining close to 100% of the better-than-world-trend performances. Hence there is little doubt that during this take-off period the predominant roots of the remarkable export performance observed during this period originated from supply factors internal to the NICs.

THE RECESSION DECADE, 1973–1982

World trade suffered a serious setback as the growth rates of world demand for products declined across the board during the period commencing with the OPEC I and ending with OPEC II world energy shocks. The average annual rate of growth of OECD-manufactured imports dropped from 18.9% to 12.3%. The growth of NIC exports (starting, to be sure, from an appreciably higher base than the middle 1960s) also fell (with the exception of Hong Kong). Nevertheless, all four NICs' exports grew at rates exceeding world import growth and hence continued to increase their market shares during this period.

What roles did the market and commodity effects play during this period? Again, a large potential existed for these factors to exert a major role, since the period was characterized by large fluctuations and changes in world markets. The period may be seen to comprise two distinct subperiods, the sharp decline into recession from 1973 to 1975 and the somewhat sluggish recovery through 1978—when the second world slump began in 1979.

From 1974 to 1975, OECD-manufactured imports actually declined by close to 1%. While EC imports increased by 3.4%, U.S. imports declined by 7%, and Japan's declined by a full 20.6%. The collapsing markets of the United States and Japan had an especially detrimental effect for South Korea and Taiwan, whose exports were heavily targeted to these two markets, as seen in Table 3.8.

Both South Korea and Taiwan had considerably diversified their marketing away from the United States toward Japan as compared to the situation in 1965 (see Table 3.5), yet they found themselves in a position where close to 80% of their respective exports were being directed to these two declining markets. In fact, as seen in Table

Table 3.8 Market Distribution of NIC Exports, 1974 (%)

Destination	South Korea	Taiwan	Singapore	Hong Kong
U.S.	48.5	63.8	55.0	48.3
EC	15.2	19.3	36.3	45.0
Japan	36.3	16.9	8.6	6.6

Table 3.9 Constant Market Share Analysis, 1975 (annual changes)

Measure	South Korea	Taiwan	Singapore	Hong Kong
Greater than world trend	−2.9	−9.8	4.2	4.7
Commodity composition effect	4.0	5.0	4.6	6.5
Market distribution effect	−13.9	−9.1	−5.5	−4.1
Competitiveness effect	7.1	−5.7	5.2	2.3

3.9, the market effects of South Korea and Taiwan were notably negative, and their overall export expansion failed to match world trends during this year.

In contrast to the market distribution effect (or market effect), the four NICs were relatively well positioned with respect to the commodity composition effect (or commodity effect). Table 3.10 presents their respective commodity specializations in 1974 plus the world rate of growth in trade (OECD imports) by commodity from 1974 to 1975. From the last column of the table it is seen that the products whose world markets suffered the greatest declines during the 1975 recession were nonferrous metals (−42%), textiles (−28%), and metal manufactures (−14%). The first four columns indicate that as the four NICs entered the mid-1970s recession, none of these products played a significant role in their respective exports, with the single exception of textiles. And even with respect to this product category, a comparison

Table 3.10 Distribution of NIC Exports for 1974 and Growth in World Imports by Product Group, 1974–75

Product Group	Percentage of NIC Exports				OECD Import Growth (%)
	Taiwan	South Korea	Singapore	Hong Kong	
Chemicals	2.4	2.3	3.3	0.5	−11.6
Metal manufactures	4.7	13.5	1.1	2.7	−13.6
Nonferrous metals	0.2	0.4	0.3	0.4	−41.9
Textiles	7.0	10.4	2.2	7.5	−27.8
Nonelectrical machinery	2.4	2.0	7.6	2.2	8.6
Electrical machinery	24.3	14.1	54.2	14.8	−8.6
Transport equipment	1.6	0.5	1.5	0.4	−4.8
Precision instruments	0.6	0.6	5.2	1.1	−3.0
Clothing	23.8	28.6	12.3	43.7	9.3
Furniture	1.5	0.4	0.6	0.7	−9.8
Footwear	7.7	5.9	0.1	1.4	12.1
Resource-based products	9.2	10.1	5.8	3.2	−8.9
Miscellaneous manufactures	14.6	11.4	5.7	22.3	−11.3

with Table 3.6 indicates that all of the NICs had significantly lessened their dependence on textiles since the mid-1960s. This shift away from textiles was especially notable for Singapore, whose proportion of textiles in all exports declined from 14.5% in 1966 to 2.2% in 1974. In addition, there had occurred a significant shift toward products that did relatively well in the mid-1970s slump. These include electrical machinery (notably for Singapore and Taiwan), and clothing (for all except Singapore). In fact, the commodity effect was positive, boosting the export performance of all four NICs in 1975.

RECESSION VERSUS EXPANSION IN THE 1970s

This section presents and discusses five-year period (four-year lags) cumulative constant market share analyses for the following periods:

1971–75   the period leading into the mid-1970s recession (Table 3.11)
1974–78   the period of relative recovery (Table 3.12)
1978–82   the period leading into the 1982 recession (Table 3.13)

This will allow us to determine how the export performance of the various NICs evolved over this period, and how each reacted to the upturn and downturns in the world economy during this period.

Several interesting patterns are revealed in Tables 3.11 to 3.13. First, the 1970s clearly was a decade in which the export performance of both South Korea and Taiwan suffered a setback relative to world trade trends. Whereas in the earlier period (1971–75) South Korea's exports expanded over three times faster than (lagging) world trade trends and Taiwan's grew by roughly double the world rate, by the end of the period (1978–82) South Korea's exports grew faster than world trends by only 17% and Taiwan's by 45%. Thus while still increasing their market shares, this behavior seemed to be approaching logistically an upper asymptotic limit. Singapore, on the other hand, seemed nowhere near such a limit, as its performance relative to world import markets continued systematically to improve throughout the period.

Of all the NICs, Hong Kong's export performance seemed most affected by world cyclical forces, expanding roughly 20% above world trends during economic turndown and roughly 40% during the inter-OPEC shock period. Neither the changes in growth (relative to world trends) of the other NICs nor the behavior of the com-

Table 3.11 Constant Market Share Analysis, 1971–75 (cumulative percentage)

Measure	South Korea	Taiwan	Singapore	Hong Kong
Greater than world trend	275.9	117.4	4.2	24.4
Commodity composition effect	4.0	7.5	4.6	8.0
Market distribution effect	−11.5	−15.3	−5.5	−8.7
Competitiveness effect	283.4	125.1	5.2	25.2

Table 3.12 Constant Market Share Analysis, 1974–78 (cumulative percentage)

Measure	South Korea	Taiwan	Singapore	Hong Kong
Greater than world trend	93.6	89.4	57.0	54.1
Commodity composition effect	4.2	7.5	6.4	9.1
Market distribution effect	−3.3	2.4	3.6	1.9
Competitiveness effect	92.6	79.5	47.0	43.2

Table 3.13 Constant Market Share Analysis, 1978–82 (cumulative percentage)

Measure	South Korea	Taiwan	Singapore	Hong Kong
Greater than world trend	17.7	45.2	74.4	23.6
Commodity composition effect	−0.7	1.5	4.6	2.8
Market distribution effect	6.5	7.7	6.1	3.7
Competitiveness effect	11.9	36.0	63.7	17.1

modity and market effects seemed especially sensitive to the cycle. The commodity effect was positive and relatively important at the beginning of the period in each of the four NICs and tended to decrease in relative importance throughout the period. By the end of the period (1978–82) the product composition of each NIC's product specialization was not an important factor in either helping or hindering the NIC export drive.

The picture is different—and in a way exactly the reverse—with respect to the market effect. The period began with negative market effects hampering the export growth performance of each of the NICs. In relative terms, being concentrated in relatively slow-growing markets was especially detrimental to Singapore and Hong Kong in the 1971–75 period. During the interim, recovery period of 1974–78, the market effect turned positive for all except South Korea. By 1978–82, the market effect became positive for all the NICs. The locational dimension of their exports became not just a positive factor but significantly positive. This was especially true for South Korea, whose market effect accounted for 37% (6.5/17.7) of its success in exceeding the world trade growth rate by 17.7%.

To understand the underlying trends that are summarized by this market effect, we present the average annual growth rates of the three major markets (all manufactured imports) for the three five-year periods under discussion and the distribution of NIC exports to these three at the end of the period (Table 3.14). The results in Table

Table 3.14 Annual Growth of OECD Manufactured Imports (%)

Destination	1971–75	1974–78	1978–82
U.S.	14.4	17.6	9.0
EC	21.1	15.0	5.2
Japan	20.3	8.4	10.9
OECD	19.3	15.3	6.6

3.14 indicate that the 1970s represented a period in which the lack of fiscal coordination was clearly reflected in the lack of cyclical coordination in the imports of the major three groups within the OECD. For the United States, imports indeed grew faster in the recovery period between the OPEC shocks and then (the growth rate) plummeted sharply in the second OPEC shock period. The EC's import growth declined in the intershock period and then continued to decline. In a sense, the 1970s were one long recession for the EC. Japan exhibited a pattern that was exactly the reverse of that of the United States. Its import growth rate declined in the middle period, and then—when those of both the United States and the EC reached their nadir—Japan's recovery began.

In light of this lack of cyclical coordination in these OECD import series, it is impossible to draw any cycle-based inferences from the CMS results cited previously. On the other hand, some light may be cast on the changing (and improving) market effects noted earlier by examining the market distribution of the NICs' exports during this period. The source of South Korea's and Taiwan's increasingly positive market effects becomes clear from the figures in Table 3.15. Both were relatively more heavily focused on the U.S. and Japanese markets than were Singapore and Hong Kong. As the decade proceeded, both the U.S. (especially from 1974 to 1978) and the Japanese import markets (1978–82) grew rapidly relative to the EC. The increasingly positive market effects of Hong Kong and Singapore may also be attributed to the fact that their relative focus on the U.S. market, though smaller than those of South Korea and Taiwan, still exceeds the relative weight of the United States in overall OECD imports (roughly half of the EC in 1982).

A close examination of the detailed constant market share tables in Appendix Table 3.1 reveals another pattern that appears to be fairly systematic and robust. In the earlier period, beginning in 1973, the competitiveness effect tended to exceed the greater-than-world-trend measure. This was true for all except Singapore, and it applied to Singapore as well in the years preceding 1973–77. In the latter part of the decade into the early 1980s, the relative weight of the supply-related competitiveness effect dropped dramatically. This finding may be interpreted as implying that the success of the NICs to continue their expansion of world market shares in the slowly expanding world markets of the late 1970s resulted more from propitious destination targeting and fortunate product specialization patterns than had hitherto been true. Until that period, the major source of success in the continued expansion of international market shares was a competitive ability to expand shares product by product and market by market, despite the handicaps of poor initial destination and commodity patterns. Thus in the latter period the NICs were suc-

Table 3.15 Market Distribution of NIC Exports, 1982 (%)

Destination	South Korea	Taiwan	Singapore	Hong Kong
U.S.	56.0	71.2	59.6	57.1
EC	21.1	18.2	32.8	38.1
Japan	22.9	10.6	7.6	4.8

Though this table is for 1982, the picture is representative of the situation throughout the previous decade, which changed only very slowly.

ceeding largely because the products in which they specialized and the markets in which they sold them both grew relatively fast.

The potential danger is clear. In the absence of an all-knowing, clairvoyant MITI, the inability to score competitive gains (at the expense of other exporters) in times of rapidly shifting markets and rapidly changing product developments creates a strong potential to fall off the winning horse. The products and markets which are today's winners may easily become tomorrow's losers. The lesson was aptly demonstrated in the mid-1970s and 1980s for those countries heavily dependent on the "winner" oil and petroleum products. As is discussed in the next section, the danger suggested by the developing trends of the 1970s came to roost by the late 1980s.

THE 1980s

What happened in the late 1980s? The cumulative constant market share for the period 1982–86 is presented in Table 3.16. We note that the disturbing pattern seen in the later 1970s was present in the mid- to late 1980s as well. The continued success of the NICs (except Hong Kong) in substantially exceeding world trade trends was significantly a function of their market effect. This was especially true for Taiwan and Singapore, both of which had a relatively high concentration of exports to the relatively rapidly growing U.S. market during this period. The phenomenon is well illustrated for the case of Hong Kong. From 1982 to 1986, Hong Kong managed to (barely) match the expansion of world trade. However, this was not due to Hong Kong's ability to supplant competitors in particular product–destination markets. Indeed, its competitiveness effect was negative! Its continued success is seen to have been solely due to fortuitous marketing patterns.

By the last third of the 1980s, all the NICs, with the noted exception of Singapore, lost market shares in the OECD-manufactured import markets. An examination of Appendix Table 3.1 reveals that this was due not to poor commodity or market positioning but rather to poor (in fact negative) competitiveness effects. That is, the NICs began demonstrating a decided weakness precisely in the ability which had catapulted them into their remarkable export drive in the mid-1960s—the ability to compete on a product-by-product and market-by-market level. Given this poor supply-related behavior, the NICs must now rely much more heavily on world demand factors—which, as noted, have tended to be fickle and cyclical and in any case have never been under the control of the NICs.

Table 3.16 Constant Market Share Analysis, 1982–86 (cumulative percentage)

Measure	South Korea	Taiwan	Singapore	Hong Kong
Greater than world trend	51.6	63.7	45.4	2.5
Commodity composition effect	−0.1	3.0	5.9	5.0
Market distribution effect	4.9	10.0	7.0	6.8
Competitiveness effect	46.7	50.7	32.6	−9.3

Appendix Table 3.1 Annual Constant Market Share Analysis Among the Four NICs, 1965–1990 (annual percentage)

	South Korea				
	1966	1967	1968	1969	1970
Greater than world trend	43.30	45.57	49.48	32.02	27.09
Commodity composition	−2.11	−4.21	0.12	3.26	−3.02
Market destination	0.09	4.74	3.84	−3.33	1.01
Competitiveness	45.31	47.04	45.52	32.09	29.09
	1971	1972	1973	1974	1975
Greater than world trend	15.62	38.36	70.96	24.27	−2.86
Commodity composition	4.98	3.66	0.57	−3.49	3.99
Market destination	−5.10	2.13	2.73	−2.18	−13.93
Competitiveness	15.74	32.56	67.66	29.94	7.08
	1976	1977	1978	1979	1980
Greater than world trend	45.14	2.72	10.63	−2.59	−9.8
Commodity composition	1.19	−0.52	0.98	−1.11	−1.85
Market destination	5.47	−1.84	5.57	−2.66	−5.77
Competitiveness	38.48	5.08	4.09	1.18	−2.19
	1981	1982	1983	1984	1985
Greater than world trend	21.6	3.74	11.3	8.67	−2.68
Commodity composition	1.78	0.56	−1.90	2.08	−1.10
Market destination	11.19	2.20	2.66	8.91	−0.80
Competitiveness	8.63	0.98	10.54	−2.33	−0.78
	1986	1987	1988	1989	1990
Greater than world trend	12.41	23.66	12.26	−7.67	−19.21
Commodity composition	0.77	1.35	−1.71	−0.21	0.88
Market destination	−6.50	−1.82	2.38	1.37	−7.68
Competitiveness	18.13	24.15	−8.82	−12.41	−12.41

	Hong Kong				
	1966	1967	1968	1969	1970
Greater than world trend	5.12	3.25	1.75	7.30	−0.16
Commodity composition	−0.25	−3.17	0.68	5.61	−0.06
Market destination	1.34	0.48	2.08	−1.16	−0.92
Competitiveness	4.03	5.94	−1.01	2.86	0.83
	1971	1972	1973	1974	1975
Greater than world trend	0.96	5.97	3.45	−9.72	4.67
Commodity composition	4.17	5.97	−0.00	−4.23	6.45
Market destination	−1.35	0.07	−4.76	−0.97	−4.06
Competitiveness	−1.85	−0.07	8.21	−4.53	2.28

Appendix Table 3.1 Continued

	1976	1977	1978	1979	1980
Greater than world trend	22.61	−2.33	3.55	4.05	2.79
Commodity composition	1.98	−0.36	1.24	−1.63	−0.50
Market destination	3.53	−0.05	2.50	−4.29	−0.53
Competitiveness	17.09	−1.92	−0.19	9.97	3.82
	1981	1982	1983	1984	1985
Greater than world trend	12.64	−0.87	3.97	10.83	−11.67
Commodity composition	4.27	0.94	−0.51	2.79	0.07
Market destination	5.13	1.71	3.55	6.53	0.95
Competitiveness	3.24	−3.51	0.92	1.51	−12.69
	1986	1987	1988	1989	1990
Greater than world trend	−5.90	1.98	−4.72	−9.79	−10.84
Commodity composition	2.79	2.91	−2.79	0.77	1.20
Market destination	−4.87	−3.17	−0.76	0.04	−3.36
Competitiveness	−3.82	2.24	−10.59	−8.69	−8.69

	Taiwan				
	1966	1967	1968	1969	1970
Greater than world trend	17.62	40.14	62.45	38.44	46.62
Commodity composition	−2.13	−3.11	0.09	4.21	0.16
Market destination	2.45	1.61	4.63	−2.46	−1.35
Competitiveness	17.3	41.63	57.73	36.69	48.81
	1971	1972	1973	1974	1975
Greater than world trend	36.82	44.72	34.04	−2.33	−9.76
Commodity composition	4.29	4.37	0.73	−3.71	5.01
Market destination	−2.61	0.16	−3.55	−1.71	−9.09
Competitiveness	35.14	40.19	36.86	3.09	−5.68
	1976	1977	1978	1979	1980
Greater than world trend	33.26	6.72	24.96	4.61	1.71
Commodity composition	−1.61	0.32	1.19	−1.28	−0.75
Market destination	6.86	−0.91	4.72	−6.02	−3.57
Competitiveness	24.79	7.31	19.06	11.91	6.03
	1981	1982	1983	1984	1985
Greater than world trend	20.28	6.14	17.08	15.6	−0.51
Commodity composition	2.45	1.18	−0.24	2.05	0.11
Market destination	11.41	2.88	5.11	10.97	1.09
Competitiveness	6.42	2.08	12.22	2.58	−1.71

(*continued*)

Appendix Table 3.1 Continued

	1986	1987	1988	1989	1990
Greater than world trend	3.90	14.79	−6.54	−6.19	−17.49
Commodity composition	1.15	1.18	−0.62	−0.13	0.80
Market destination	−7.50	−7.50	−0.06	0.28	−6.46
Competitiveness	10.25	17.99	−5.87	−6.34	−11.83

		Singapore			
	1966	1967	1968	1969	1970
Greater than world trend	na	−23.24	28.41	58.36	90.34
Commodity composition	na	−4.59	−0.54	2.53	−1.63
Market destination	na	1.01	0.03	−1.89	−1.81
Competitiveness	na	−19.66	28.93	57.73	93.78

	1971	1972	1973	1974	1975
Greater than world trend	59.21	94.94	77.27	−8.22	4.21
Commodity composition	1.24	3.78	3.48	−2.87	4.57
Market destination	0.72	1.67	−4.43	−1.68	−5.50
Competitiveness	57.24	89.49	78.22	−3.67	5.15

	1976	1977	1978	1979	1980
Greater than world trend	21.51	−0.35	4.63	20.03	17.22
Commodity composition	1.39	0.18	−0.29	−1.64	1.27
Market destination	5.37	−1.64	1.44	−2.60	−0.59
Competitiveness	14.76	1.11	3.48	24.27	16.53

	1981	1982	1983	1984	1985
Greater than world trend	14.26	3.27	16.12	21.71	−9.47
Commodity composition	4.28	1.72	2.20	4.50	−0.23
Market destination	6.94	0.72	0.72	7.78	−0.28
Competitiveness	3.04	0.83	9.27	9.41	−8.97

	1986	1987	1988	1989	1990
Greater than world trend	−1.30	19.44	18.33	10.35	2.83
Commodity composition	0.48	1.67	1.40	0.62	0.47
Market destination	−4.47	−3.17	0.03	−0.26	−5.92
Competitiveness	2.70	20.99	9.98	9.98	8.28

Appendix Table 3.2   Cumulative Five-Year Constant Market Share Analysis (%)

Measure	1965–70	1970–75	1975–80	1980–85	1985–90
		South Korea			
Greater than world trend	719.0	387.3	128.9	55.8	52.5
Commodity composition	−10.5	8.2	−1.7	1.1	1.4
Market destination	3.8	−16.0	2.2	19.4	−15.1
Competitiveness	725.7	395.2	128.4	35.4	66.2
		Hong Kong			
Greater than world trend	58.9	37.7	104.8	15.9	−21.8
Commodity composition	2.2	11.5	−0.1	7.0	4.9
Market destination	1.7	−11.2	2.3	11.7	−17.0
Competitiveness	55.1	37.5	102.6	−2.8	−9.7
		Taiwan			
Greater than world trend	736.5	246.0	208.8	80.8	0.6
Commodity composition	−8.4	10.9	0.2	5.1	2.2
Market destination	−0.8	−15.6	3.1	27.0	−22.8
Competitiveness	745.7	250.7	205.5	48.7	21.2
		Singapore			
Greater than world trend	602.1	711.8	191.1	56.6	128.2
Commodity composition	1.2	8.3	1.1	11.2	4.4
Market destination	−2.9	−9.9	4.3	15.0	−15.6
Competitiveness	603.7	713.4	185.7	30.4	139.4

NOTES

1. E. E. Leamer and R. M. Stern, *Quantitative International Economics* (Boston: Allyn and Bacon, 1970).

2. In this section OECD refers solely to the United States, Japan, and the original EC countries plus the United Kingdom.

3. The exogeneity of the market effect, as well as the commodity effect, is an especially credible hypothesis during the 1980s, when it was observed (e.g., see Table 3.5) that compositional changes in NIC exports were relatively slight.

REFERENCES

Leamer, E. E., and R. M. Stern. 1970. *Quantitative International Economics*. Boston: Allyn and Bacon.

4

Export Patterns: Who's Ahead?

To further explore whether the four little tigers have been gaining on or falling behind Japan, in this chapter we compare the export performance of the four Asian NICs with that of Japan. The criterion used here is the "similarity index" of Finger and Kreinin (1972).[1]

SIMILARITIES WITH JAPAN

Japan represents a fascinating role model to the East Asian NICs. Following a disastrous defeat, Japan rose in a few short decades to become a world economic superpower. This persistent and convincing economic triumph tends to present a powerful example to be emulated, even in the face of historical animosities found in South Korea and, to a lesser degree, in Taiwan.

Clearly the institutional details, including such factors as interlocking Kereitsu and MITI, are not easily transferable although some clear examples exist of conscious emulation of the Japanese institutional model, at least in South Korea.[2] Table 4.1 presents empirical "revealed" evidence of a clear tendency for the NICs to try to approximate and copy the Japanese export pattern since the mid-1960s, when the former began to take off.

The figures in Table 4.1 indicate that the proportional export compositions of the four NICs were somewhat similar to that of Japan in the mid-1960s. During the following 25 years, Singapore's exports continued to be statistically similar to those of Japan. That is, as Japan's dynamic comparative advantage shifted, that of Singapore tended to match these shifts. This was clearly not the case with the other three NICs. By 1970 two of the four NICs had an export makeup that was not at all significantly correlated with that of Japan. By 1980 this was true of all the NICs except Singapore. If we accept as a conceptual working hypothesis that Japan served as a role model to be emulated by the NICs, then clearly by the early 1980s the latter were slipping further and further behind that goal. Only by 1990 were the export compositions of all the NICs (except Hong Kong) again significantly correlated with that of Japan (and the correlation coefficients tended to be higher than they had been in the mid-1960s).

Table 4.1 Correlation Coefficients
Between NICs' and Japan's Export
Compositions, Selected Years

	1965	1970	1980	1990
South Korea	0.32[a]	0.17	0.09	0.40[a]
Taiwan	0.32[a]	0.33[a]	0.13	0.39[a]
Singapore	0.28[a]	0.24[a]	0.24[a]	0.42[a]
Hong Kong	0.38[a]	0.13	0.04	0.09

[a]Significant at the 95% level.

The Pearson correlation coefficient does not directly measure the degree of mutual overlap of product compositions. An intuitively appealing measure of the degree of emulation of the Japanese export pattern is the similarity index, as described in Finger and Kreinin. This indicator measures the degree of export-vector overlap. Thus if two countries exported mutually exclusive categories of products (as would be the case with the complete specialization in the classic Ricardian two-country model), with no product overlap, the similarity index would take on the value of 0. If two countries exported (proportionally) identical product categories, the index would equal 1. An index of 0.5 would indicate that an overlap existed for 50% of the products.

The increase in similarity with Japan's exports is clear. In the mid-1960s, this measure ranged from a low of only a 19% product overlap for Singapore (which thus differed considerably in export composition from Japan), to a high of 35% for Taiwan. By the late 1980s, the range was from a *low* of 35% for Hong Kong, which thus shifted from being most similar to Japan to least similar, to a high of over 50% for South Korea. The shift to becoming closer in composition to Japan was especially notable in the cases of Singapore and South Korea.

THE DYNAMICS OF THE SHIFTS IN COMPARATIVE ADVANTAGE: SETTLING THE PARADOX

A certain conceptual problem arises as a result of the preceding analysis. If indeed it is true that over time the NICs are progressively simulating Japan in their respective export patterns, then it would seem to follow that they should be found to be progressively displacing Japan in world markets. However, recent studies found this not to be the case.[3]

One way to settle this apparent paradox is to consider the dynamic relationship between export patterns of the NICs and of Japan over time in terms of a moving target—that is, a dynamic concept of changing comparative advantage over time.[4] It may be considered that at any point in time the NICs are indeed approaching Japan's patterns as they are perceived at that time.[5] Meanwhile, Japan's trade composition and pattern of comparative advantage are changing—often quite rapidly.[6] Thus at any point in time the trade pattern of any given NIC may be asymptotically approaching the pattern that had characterized *past* Japanese trade vectors. In such a case, it may well be found that *at any given time,* no actual NIC displacement of Japan's export shares is occurring.

The following four sets of graphs illustrate this dynamic concept empirically. Each graph presents the similarity indices between a NIC's exports in 1965, 1970, 1980, and 1990 and those of Japan in one particular year. If indeed it is true that the NICs are "chasing" Japan, then in any given year we should expect to find the highest similarity for any given NIC export vector to be with a past period's Japanese export vector. If, for example, over the 25 years examined a country's export pattern is continually growing more similar to Japan's 1965 pattern, then one would expect to find a monotonically increasing line on a graph showing the similarity index between that country's export patterns for 1965, 1970, and 1990 and Japan's for 1965.

Figures 4.1 through 4.4 illustrate the relationships between Korea's exports throughout the 25-year period and a given year's export composition of Japan. The findings here support the hypothesis that throughout this period Korea's evolving pattern of revealed comparative advantage was (asymptotically) approaching and approximating Japanese patterns of past years. Thus Figure 4.1 indicates the similarity indices between South Korea's exports in various years and those of Japan in 1965. We note that the hypothesis is indeed supported by the findings. The highest degree of product overlap is always found between Korea's exports at any given point in time and those of Japan in a lagged, or past, period. Thus we find that the degree of similarity between Japan's 1965 export pattern and Korea's 1965 export pattern is very slight (Figure 4.1 and Table 4.2). However, Korea's 1970 exports (Figure 4.2) involve a sharply increased degree of similarity with Japan's 1965 pattern. The similarity with Japan's 1965 export composition increases with Korea's export patterns of 1980 (Figure 4.3) and even more so in 1990 (Figure 4.4). Thus, 25 years later, Korea's export specialization pattern resembled that of Japan's pattern of 1965 better than it had in any of the preceding years.

The second set of diagrams (Figures 4.5–4.8) describe the same respective relations between Taiwan and Japan. The pattern is similar, with some minor variations. As in the case of Korea, Japan's 1965 export pattern is most closely approximated by Taiwan's patterns of later years. Thus the degree of similarity with Japan's 1965 (and with Japan's 1970) exports increases over time. Taiwan's 1970 exports are more similar to Japan's 1965 pattern than is Taiwan's 1965 pattern; and Taiwan's 1980 pattern is most closely similar to that of Japan's 1965 (and 1970) trade compositional pattern. An interesting difference between Korea and Taiwan is re-

Table 4.2 Similarity Index Between NICs' and Japan's Exports, 1965 and 1990 (%)

	1965	1990
South Korea	29.0	51.4
Taiwan	35.1	46.9
Singapore	19.2	45.8
Hong Kong	34.3	34.7

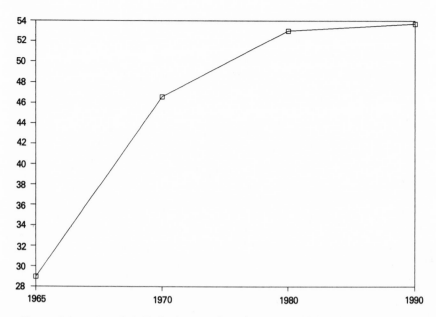

Figure 4.1   Index of similarity between Korea's exports and Japan's 1965 exports.

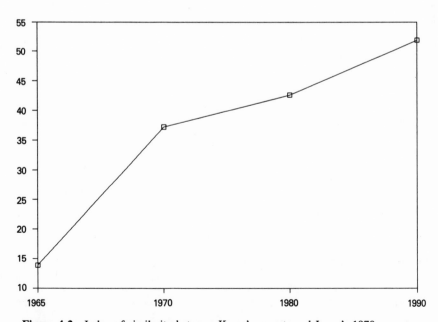

Figure 4.2   Index of similarity between Korea's exports and Japan's 1970 exports.

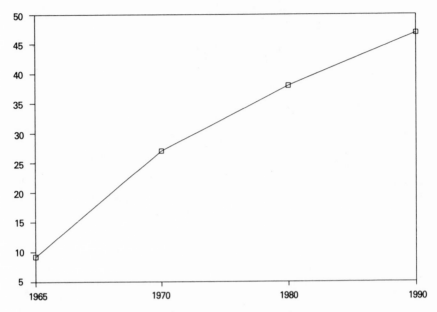

Figure 4.3 Index of similarity between Korea's exports and Japan's 1980 exports.

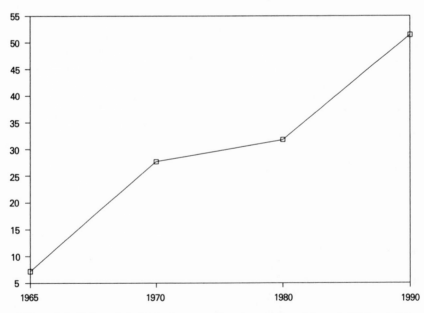

Figure 4.4 Index of similarity between Korea's exports and Japan's 1990 exports.

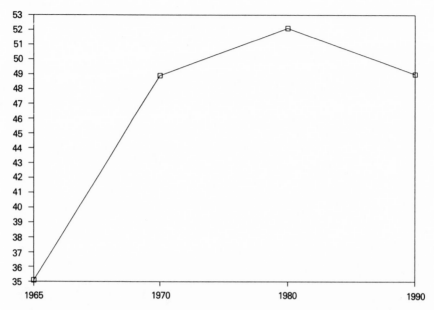

Figure 4.5 Index of similarity between Taiwan's exports and Japan's 1965 exports.

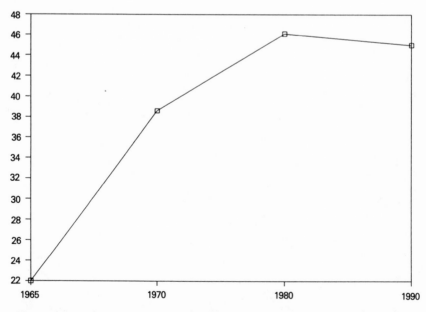

Figure 4.6 Index of similarity between Taiwan's exports and Japan's 1970 exports.

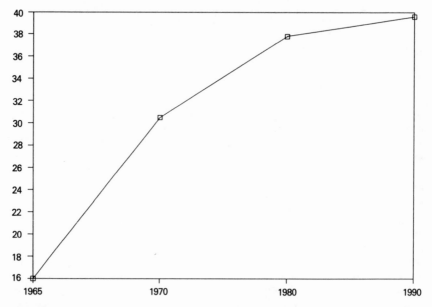

Figure 4.7 Index of similarity between Taiwan's exports and Japan's 1980 exports.

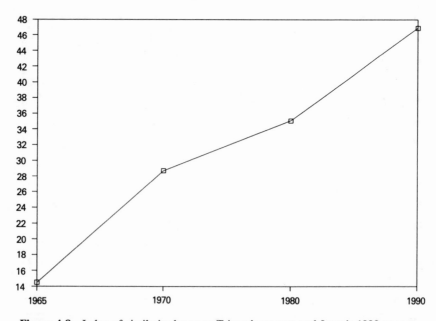

Figure 4.8 Index of similarity between Taiwan's exports and Japan's 1990 exports.

vealed with respect to their respective 1990 trade pattern. Compared with Taiwan's 1980 pattern, Taiwan's 1990 exports were less similar to Japan's 1965 and 1970 export composition. This can be seen in Figures 4.5 and 4.6, where the slope of the line connecting the various similarity patterns rises through 1980 but then falls slightly from 1980 to 1990. If we interpret the monotonically rising line as indicating a continuous dynamic "catching-up" process, then the break in the slope indicates that Taiwan was still catching up with Japan's export compositional patterns of earlier years (1965 and 1970) up to 1980. By the 1980s, however, Taiwan had caught up and surpassed Japan's export patterns of those earlier years. However, the monotonically increasing patterns found in Figure 4.7 indicate that by 1980 Taiwan had not yet caught up with the contemporary Japanese pattern. When Japan's 1980 exports are compared with Taiwan's, they are found to be most similar *not* with Taiwan's 1980 patterns, but rather with that of a decade later, 1990 (Figure 4.8).

Figures 4.9 to 4.12 present the results for the case of Singapore. Here too a catching-up thesis is supported by the patterns revealed. However, the catching up is seen to have occurred more rapidly than it had for either Korea or Taiwan. As was true for Taiwan, when compared with Japan's export compositions of 1965 and 1970, the turning point in the rising similarity pattern occurs between 1980 and 1990. However, unlike Taiwan, Figure 4.11, which compares Singapore's exports with Japan's 1980 pattern, also indicates a drop in the similarity index between 1980 and 1990. This indicates that by 1980 Singapore had essentially caught up with Japan. Japan's 1980 export pattern was most similar to that of Singapore in 1980 rather than 1990 (Figure 4.12), as was true for Taiwan and the others. From this two

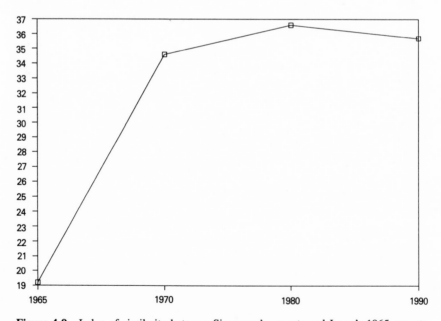

Figure 4.9 Index of similarity between Singapore's exports and Japan's 1965 exports.

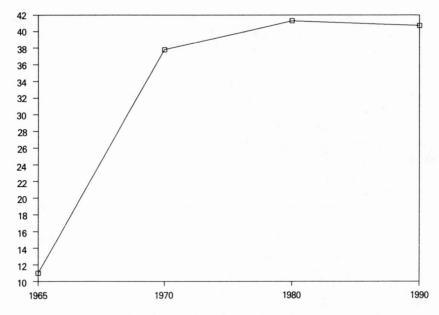

Figure 4.10 Index of similarity between Singapore's exports and Japan's 1970 exports.

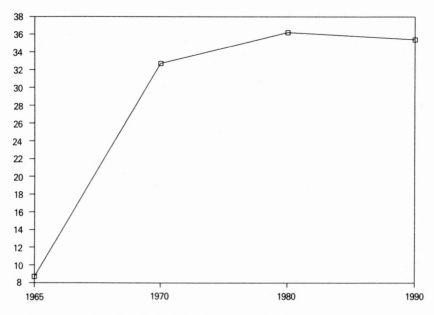

Figure 4.11 Index of similarity between Singapore's exports and Japan's 1980 exports.

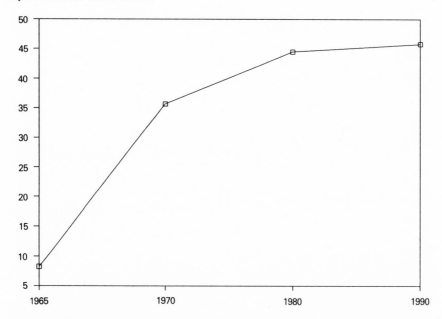

Figure 4.12 Index of similarity between Singapore's exports and Japan's 1990 exports.

important inferences may be made. First, in terms of the "catching up with Japan" thesis, of the three NICs studied to this point, Singapore clearly came closest—and had essentially reached equality by the early 1980s. The other is that from that point on—during the 1980s and into the 1990s—this catching-up model was not likely to be descriptive or analytically useful for the case of Singapore.

Figures 4.13 to 4.16 extend the same analysis to Hong Kong. Here the intertemporal pattern is more complicated. From the first diagram of this group, Figure 4.13, we see that like all the other NICs, Hong Kong better approximated Japan's 1965 pattern with that of a lagged year, 1970. However, beyond this the results diverge from the others, as the intertemporal line turns negative after 1970. This indicates that Hong Kong most closely resembled Japan's 1965 pattern in 1970. In terms of our model, Hong Kong had caught up with 1965 Japan only five years later. This performance outstripped even that of Singapore. However, when we turn to Figures 4.14 through 4.16, we find only continuously rising lines. Like Korea, this would indicate that though Hong Kong had reached its point of closest similarity with 1965 Japan by 1970, it then proceeded to slowly approach Japan's pattern of 1970—and did not succeed in approximating that year's pattern at least until 1990. This would suggest that systematic transformations in its export patterns, following Japan's leadership, slowed down after the early 1970s.

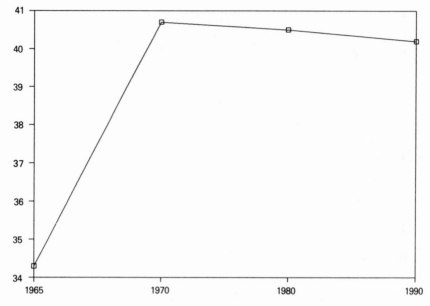

Figure 4.13   Index of similarity between Hong Kong's exports and Japan's 1965 exports.

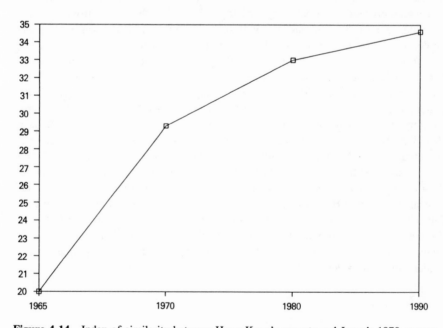

Figure 4.14   Index of similarity between Hong Kong's exports and Japan's 1970 exports.

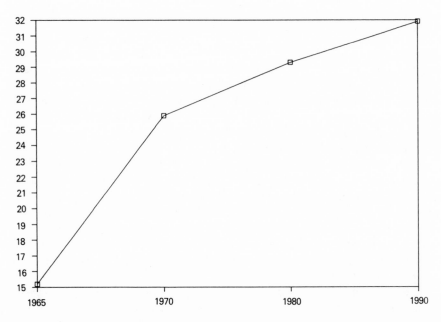

Figure 4.15 Index of similarity between Hong Kong's exports and Japan's 1980 exports.

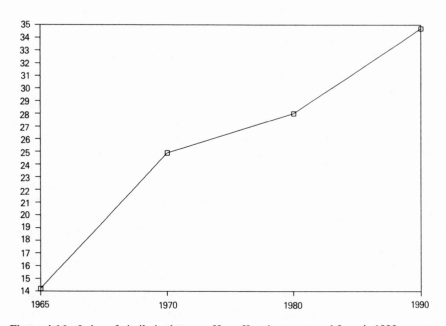

Figure 4.16 Index of similarity between Hong Kong's exports and Japan's 1990 exports.

LEADERS AND LAGGERS: ANOTHER LOOK

Between 1965 and 1990 the four NICs not only were rapidly expanding their exports but also were experiencing rapid compositional changes in their export product specialization patterns. The preceding section explored the hypothesis that these changes reflected a systematic "pursuit" of Japan's export composition pattern. In this section we ask a different question: Using solely evidence from the NICs themselves, can one say which of them was "leading" and which "lagging" in the transformational "race to modernity"?

In this section, we again utilize the graphical interperiod similarity index comparison method to answer this question. Comparisons are drawn between Singapore and Hong Kong and between Taiwan and Korea. The remaining three possible pairwise comparisons are omitted, since Hong Kong and Singapore have an essentially unique economic structure. Both are relatively small. Both are entrepôt city-states, with no agricultural (or other primary) base. Hence both are different from Taiwan and Korea, rendering the results of any comparison between these two groups of doubtful usefulness.

As was done in the preceding section, the analysis was pursued comparing export similarity indices between each pair of countries, holding one country and year constant while varying the period associated with the other. To illustrate with an example, we compare South Korea's exports in 1965, 1970, 1980, and 1990 with Taiwan's exports in 1970. We ask the following question: Which year's exports of South Korea are most similar to Taiwan's 1970 export composition? Suppose the answer were found to be 1965. This would suggest that South Korea is the "leader" for this pair of countries and years. If, on the other hand, the answer were 1980, then South Korea could be adduced to be following Taiwan's leadership in this regard.

In order to make sense of the findings in the diagrams that follow, the underlying model must be made clear. The working assumption is that the NICs (Taiwan and Korea on the one hand, Singapore and Hong Kong on the other) were all moving through significant shifts in their respective export product compositions during the period studied. Further, they were all moving generally in a convergence pattern, tending to asymptotically approximate past patterns characteristic of Japan. If it is found that one NIC's export composition is most similar to a past (rather than contemporaneous or future) pattern of another, then we would conclude that the first is following, or lagging behind, the second.

The first set of four diagrams, Figures 4.17 through 4.20, show the changing relationship over time between Taiwan's and Korea's mutual similarity indices. These diagrams lead to the general conclusion that though there was no indication of a lead or a lag in 1965, by 1970 it becomes clear that Taiwan began to lead (and Korea to lag).

In Figures 4.17 through 4.24 we note monotonically falling lines, indicating that the export pattern most similar to Korea's 1965 pattern was Taiwan's 1965 export composition pattern (and vice versa). However, Figure 4.22 indicates that Korea's 1980 pattern was most similar to Taiwan's 1970 exports. Thus by 1970 Taiwan had pulled ahead and was leading Korea. Figure 4.19 indicates that this lead–lag pattern

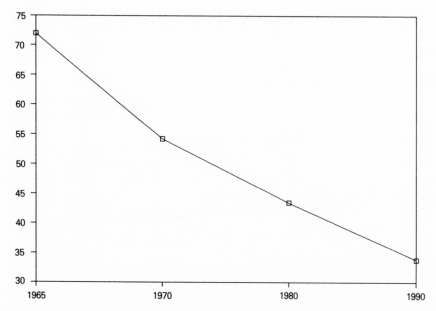

Figure 4.17 Similarity between Taiwan's exports and Korea's 1965 exports.

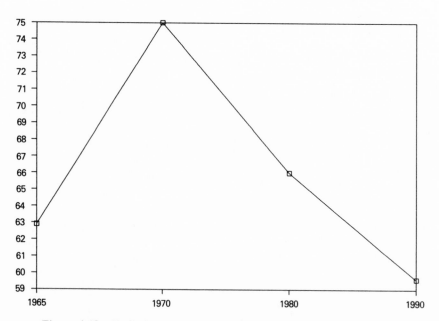

Figure 4.18 Similarity between Taiwan's exports and Korea's 1970 exports.

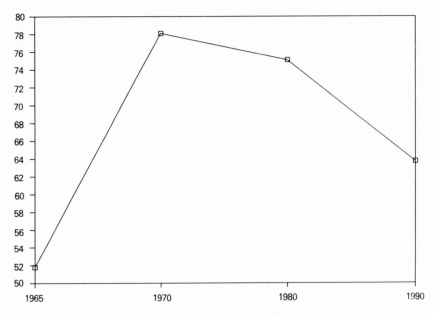

Figure 4.19 Similarity between Taiwan's exports and Korea's 1980 exports.

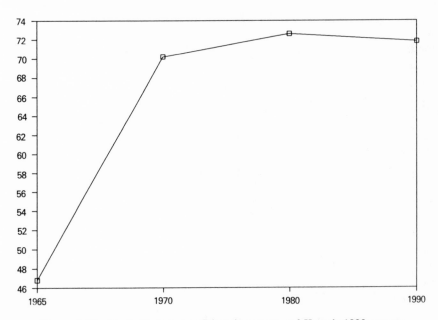

Figure 4.20 Similarity between Taiwan's exports and Korea's 1990 exports.

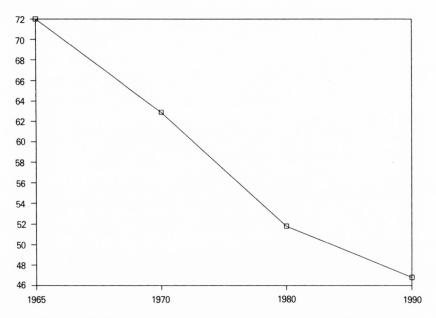

Figure 4.21   Similarity between Korea's exports and Taiwan's 1965 exports.

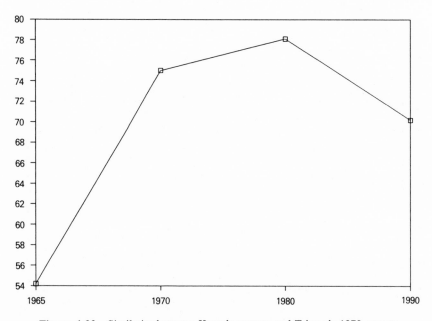

Figure 4.22   Similarity between Korea's exports and Taiwan's 1970 exports.

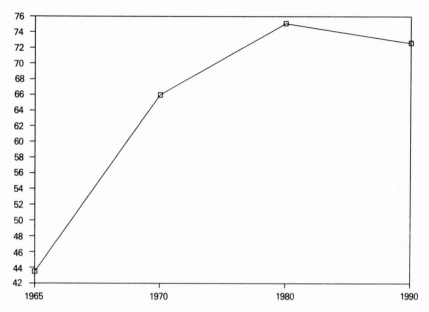

Figure 4.23 Similarity between Korea's exports and Taiwan's 1980 exports.

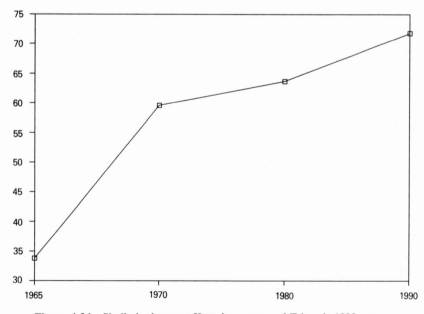

Figure 4.24 Similarity between Korea's exports and Taiwan's 1990 exports.

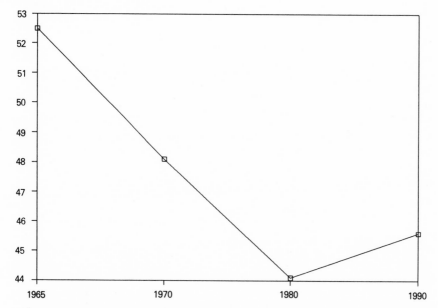

Figure 4.25   Similarity between Hong Kong's exports and Singapore's 1965 exports.

continued into the 1980s. Here we note that Korea's 1980 exports were most similar to those of Taiwan in 1970. Finally, from Figure 4.20 we see that the lead–lag pattern remains somewhat descriptive as late as the early 1990s, as Korea's 1990 exports are found to be most similar to Taiwan's 1980 exports.

Figures 4.25 through 4.32 describe the relationship between Singapore's and Hong Kong's exports during the same time period. Again, in Figures 4.25 and 4.29, as before, we find the 1965 patterns to be contemporaneous in nature. However, beginning in 1970 Singapore surges ahead and takes up a clear leading position. In Figure 4.26 Singapore's 1970 exports are most similar to those of Hong Kong in 1990—a lag of more than a decade. The relatively backward position of Hong Kong is verified in Figure 4.30, where Hong Kong's 1970 exports are most similar to those of Singapore of the earlier period of 1965. In Figure 4.27 Singapore's 1980 pattern is found most similar to Hong Kong's 1990; and in Figure 4.31 Hong Kong's 1980 pattern is found to be most closely similar to Singapore's of a decade earlier. Finally, Figure 4.32 verifies the earlier finding, as Hong Kong's 1990 pattern most closely approximates that of Singapore in 1970.

SUMMARY

An intertemporal examination of the respective export compositions of the four Asian NICs indicates that although they differ significantly from each other at any given time, they all share a clear dynamic tendency to emulate Japan. However,

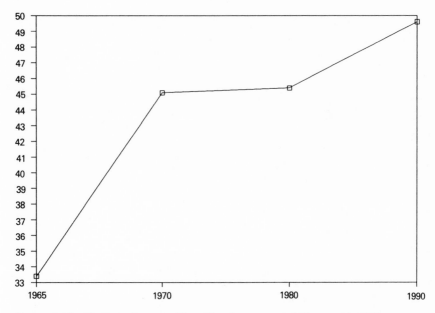

Figure 4.26   Similarity between Hong Kong's exports and Singapore's 1970 exports.

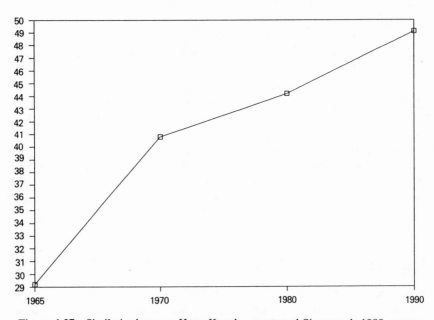

Figure 4.27   Similarity between Hong Kong's exports and Singapore's 1980 exports.

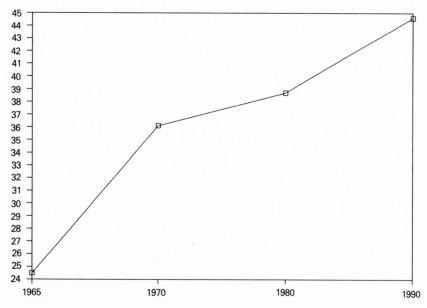

Figure 4.28 Similarity between Hong Kong's exports and Singapore's 1990 exports.

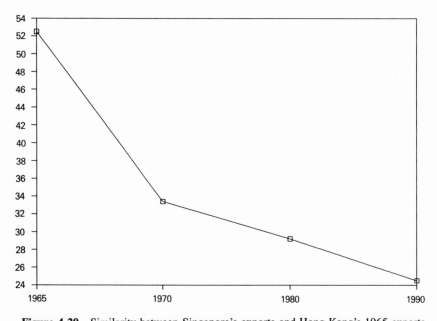

Figure 4.29 Similarity between Singapore's exports and Hong Kong's 1965 exports.

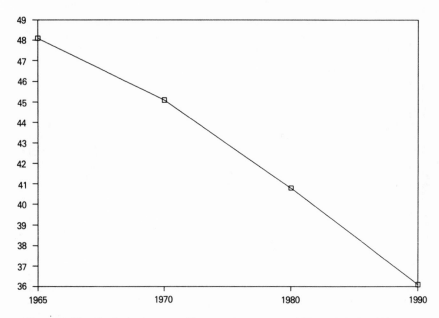

Figure 4.30 Similarity between Singapore's exports and Hong Kong's 1970 exports.

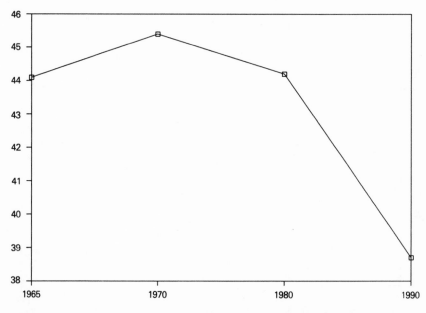

Figure 4.31 Similarity between Singapore's exports and Hong Kong's 1980 exports.

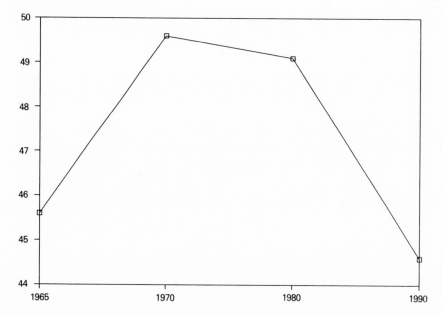

Figure 4.32 Similarity between Singapore's exports and Hong Kong's 1990 exports.

rather than match and hence displace the faster growing Japan, they demonstrate a more complex interaction. During this period the NICs systematically switched their export patterns to more closely approximate past patterns of Japan's export vector, a pattern which, except for Singapore, continues into the early 1990s. Since Japan itself was rapidly shifting the basis of its comparative advantage from a labor-intensive to a physical- and human capital–intensive basis during this period, the NICs managed to chase after Japan and yet complement, rather than directly compete with, Japan in the OECD market.

Since over most of this period the NICs' exports were growing more rapidly than those of Japan, there was a tendency to converge to Japan's concurrent export composition, and by the early 1990s over 50% of some of the NICs' exports overlapped with those of Japan.

Though all the NICs took part in this dynamic trend to emulate Japan, a complex pattern of leads and lags was noted. Hong Kong took an early lead in the last part of the 1960s but faced substantial challenges from Singapore by the 1980s. It is apparent from a periodic analysis of similarity indices made between Korea and Taiwan, that Korea, though more closely matching Japan's export pattern by the 1980s, was systematically shifting to export patterns which tended to resemble past export compositions of Taiwan.

NOTES

1. The index and some aggregation bias properties associated with it are further described in Kellman (1983).
2. The "indicative planning" in Korea and, to a lesser extent, in Taiwan is more or less imitating the Japanese planning forms. The Economic Planning Board in Korea is comparable to the Japanese MITI in its functions and arguably in its behavior.
3. See Chow (1990).
4. See Balassa (1979).
5. This study abstracts from the question of quality. At least one author argued that though the United States may appear to be importing similar products from Japan and from the NICs, in fact the former are "upmarket goods," whereas the latter are "downmarket goods." See Grossman (1982).
6. See Kellman and Landau (1984).

REFERENCES

Akamatsu, K. 1962. "A Historical Pattern of Economic Growth in Developing Countries." *Developing Economies*, no. 1 (March–August):7–13.

Balassa, Bela. 1979. "The Changing Pattern of Comparative Advantage in Manufactured Goods." *Review of Economics and Statistics* 61:259–66.

Chow, Peter C. Y. 1990. "The Revealed Comparative Advantage of the East Asian NICs." *International Trade Journal* 5, no. 2:235–62.

Finger, J., and M. Kreinin. "A Measure of 'Export Similarity' and Its Possible Uses." *Economic Journal* 89:905–12.

Grossman, Gene M. 1982. "Import Competition from Developed and Developing Countries." *Review of Economics and Statistics* 14, no. 2:271–81.

Kellman, M. 1983. "The Export Similarity Index—Some Structural Tests." *Economic Journal* (March) 93:193–98.

Kellman, Mitchell, and D. Landau. 1984. "The Nature of Japan's Comparative Advantage, 1965–80." *World Development* 12, no. 4:433–38.

5

Theoretical Underpinnings of Success

Classic Ricardian and neoclassic factor-proportions models have recently been recast in dynamic terms and applied to specific NIC cases (e.g., Balassa, 1981). Some of the recent findings are somewhat disturbing. Conventional wisdom tells us that the successful NIC export drives were primarily fueled by a reliance on a (Ricardian) specialization in labor-intensive products, following a (Heckscher–Ohlin) factor endowment–based comparative advantage. Indeed it is often stated that the export take-off of these countries was stymied by early (misguided) capital-biased import-substitution development strategies. While such industrial policy tends to succeed in promoting selected sectors ("strategic industries" in Taiwan; "favored industries" in Korea), it fails to encourage large-scale sustained export drives. It is typically argued that export success was attained by the East Asian NICs only with subsequent adoption of less capital-biased export promotion policy (or laissez-faire "hands-off" policies in the case of Hong Kong).

Recent studies (e.g., Khana), however, note a systematic increase in the share of capital-intensive exports in the case of Korea. To be sure, this apparent inconsistency may be explained in several ways. First, measurement errors may have occurred due to limited product or year coverage. This possibility will be explored by recalculating capital/labor ratio embodiments for all manufactured exports of the NICs over the 25-year period. Second, it may be that the NIC comparative advantage is based on theoretical constructs other than the classic or neoclassic models. Indeed, many new approaches have been proposed by trade economists to explain trade relationships between nations (e.g., Krugman, Linder, Vernon); many of them complement rather than replace Ricardian or neoclassical theories of comparative advantage. In such a case, the observed embodied capital intensity of the NIC exports may (merely or actually) reflect internationally increased taste similarities as per capita income differentials between the NICs and their OECD trade partners tend to shrink over time. Or perhaps the measured capital/labor embodiments may proxy for growing (capital-embodied) technological sophistication, as NIC internal markets and industrial bases grow in size and sophistication. Or it may be that, following Krugman, world *and NIC* trade has been increasing primarily in differentiated products, or in products characterized by increasing scale economies, all of which may happen to also be relatively capital intensive. In this chapter, several alternative trade theories are tested empirically to explore their respective relevance to the export performances in the NICs.[1]

PRODUCT CHARACTERISTICS EMBODIED IN NIC EXPORTS

A generally accepted theory in development economics views the dynamic development of comparative advantage of poor countries as following a well-established pattern: as a country progresses, the commodity composition of its exports will change according to its changing comparative advantage. Hence the pattern of trade and the resultant division of labor will be subject to dynamic change in a rapidly growing economy.[2] The earliest stage (recently characteristic of only certain poor countries in sub-Saharan Africa) is associated with a reliance of exports of primary—agricultural or mining—products. The second stage consists of a shift to exports of products closely associated with the available raw material—leather goods or textiles. The third stage consists of the exports of simple, labor-intensive consumer goods. The fourth stage sees a shift to more sophisticated capital goods; finally there is a shift to R&D-, or technology-intensive ("product-cycle") goods.[3] This "stages of exports" model provides a rough model against which to assess and understand the rapid changes and evolution of the NIC export compositions during the period studied here.

One way to infer the applicability of one or another underlying theory in explaining comparative advantage is to look below the surface and observe trade flows defined along dimensions of embodied factors and to find underlying characteristics. In this section we do so for the manufactured exports of all four East Asian NICs in each of the major OECD markets: the United States, the EC, and Japan. We are especially interested in noting how each of these markets differed from one another and whether the differences tended to grow or diminish during the period observed, 1965 to 1990. The implications of the observed trends to specific trade theories are then explored.

The first proposition we examine is that NIC trade tends to be consistent with or explainable by a neoclassical factor proportions model. Put succinctly, taking advantage of their relatively inexpensive labor, the East Asian NICs successfully promoted the exports of labor-intensive products.[4] This hypothesis of the source of NIC export success is examined in Figures 5.1 through 5.4. In each, the capital per worker embodied in the production process of each of the 101 manufactured exports is weighted by the actual exports in each year. Thus a rising line in a diagram would indicate a situation in which, over time, there is a shift toward more capital-intensive exports.

The results from Figures 5.1 through 5.4 indicate that the four NICs did indeed tend over time to shift to more labor-intensive products, though not to the same degree or with the same timing. Three of the four—Korea, Taiwan, and Singapore—did experience a marked shift to relatively labor-intensive products early in the period. This is evidenced by a falling level of embodied capital/labor in the graphs. Figure 5.1 shows that Korea, which started with a relatively high level of capital-intensive products, experienced a sharp and continuous shift to more labor-

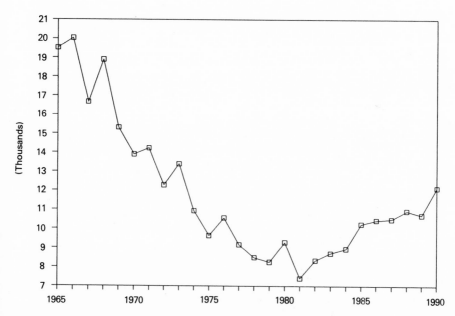

Figure 5.1 Capital/labor embodied in Korea's exports.

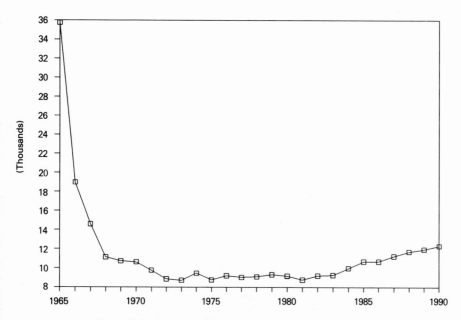

Figure 5.2 Capital/labor embodied in Taiwan's exports.

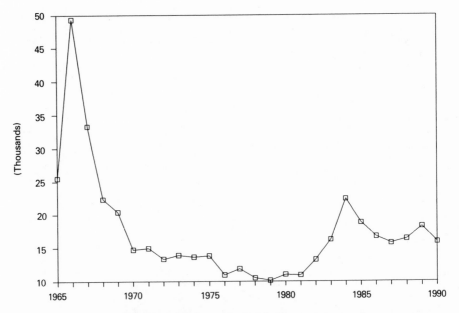

Figure 5.3   Capital/labor embodied in Singapore's exports.

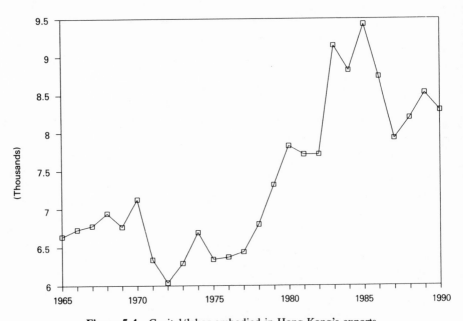

Figure 5.4   Capital/labor embodied in Hong Kong's exports.

intensive products from 1965 to the early 1980s. After that, the trend reversed, and the shift was to more capital-intensive products throughout the 1980s. Taiwan (Figure 5.2) experienced a sharper shift to more labor-intensive products, which ended around the early 1970s. After that there is a gradual (more gradual than Korea's) shift away from labor-intensive products. Singapore (Figure 5.3) experienced roughly the same type of shift. Starting with a relatively high capital-intensive export product mix, there was a gradual shift to more labor-intensive products. Like Korea, this trend was reversed in the early 1980s. As compared with the other NICs, Hong Kong (Figure 5.4) had a relatively labor-intensive export product mix in the mid-1960s. During the period, its exports remained relatively labor intensive. However, there is a noted tendency for a shift toward relatively more capital-intensive products over the entire period.

Thus the conventional view—that the NICs' export success was rooted in a continuous shift in their comparative advantage to more labor- (or less capital-) intensive product mixes—is borne out for all.[5] Hong Kong had the lowest measure of embodied capital per worker throughout the period. The other three demonstrated clear shifts in the "correct" direction (toward a less capital-intensive export product mix) from the mid-1960s to the mid- or late 1970s. From the early 1980s, however, the paradigm no longer seems supported by actual events, as all four of the NICs experienced shifts toward more capital-intensive export mixes.

Another test of the conventional thesis would be to decompose the exports by major OECD markets. It is logical to expect to find that the NICs' export compositions to Japan differ from those to the United States and to the EC. "The interdependence between the U.S. economy and the NICs differs from the relations of Europe or Japan with those countries."[6]

It is generally accepted that during this period the United States was more highly endowed in capital per worker than was the EC; in turn, the EC tended to enjoy a higher capital (per worker) endowment than Japan during most of this period. If indeed the NICs' export success was a function of their ability to exploit their relatively abundant labor endowments, one would then expect that their exports to those three markets would demonstrate a descending order of capital/labor ratio embodiment from Japan to the EC to the U.S. markets. This expectation is generally supported, as seen in Figures 5.5 through 5.8. These four graphs tend to support the stated hypothesis. For the exports of all four NICs, those destined to Japan (with the relatively low capital per worker embodiment) were most heavily weighted with highly capital-intensive products; for most of these, the United States was sent the export mixes most highly weighted with labor-intensive products.

THE PROPORTION OF CONSUMER GOODS IN THE EXPORT MIX: THE CONSUMER RATIO

The second characteristic examined is the consumer goods (CG) embodiment. In his classic study, Hufbauer noted the proportion of each three-digit (SITC Rev 1) product group which was sold directly to consumer demand. In general, each

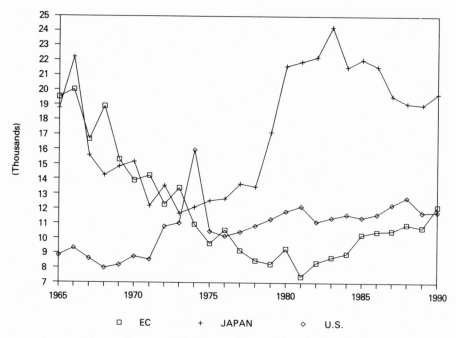

Figure 5.5   Capital/labor embodied in Korea's exports, by major OECD market.

manufactured product group consists of semiprocessed, unassembled, or capital goods and components destined to reach consumers either directly or indirectly.

As early as 1965, the United States was the biggest market for the NICs' exports of consumer goods manufactures. During the 1970s Japan, which had been importing raw materials from the NICs, shifted its sources of raw materials to the ASEAN countries and began to import manufactured consumer goods from the NICs as well. In the mid-1960s the EC imported only simple consumer goods products from the NICs (since, like the United States, the major sources for its raw materials were located elsewhere). Figures 5.9 through 5.12 describe the consumer goods ratios embodied in NIC–OECD exports.

The figures present clear evidence of a long-term shift in the OECD-bound exports of the NICs away from (simple) consumer goods to more sophisticated capital and industrial-intermediate goods. Again, a diverse pattern is observed along this dimension between the four NICs. Both Singapore (with a relatively low consumer ratio throughout) and Hong Kong (with a relatively high one) had a continuous trend of a falling consumer goods ratio throughout the period until 1985, when the shift away from consumer goods stopped for the case of Hong Kong. On the other hand, Korea and Taiwan exhibit a more complicated pattern. Both experienced a discernible increase in their embodied consumer goods ratio from the mid-1960s through the middle or late 1970s. Only since the late 1970s have they joined the others in experiencing a continuous shift away from consumer goods.

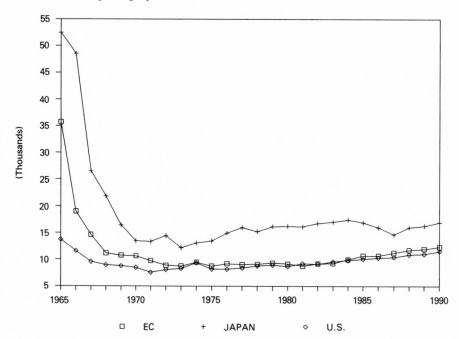

Figure 5.6 Capital/labor embodied in Taiwan's exports, by major OECD market.

An interpretation of these findings in terms of the "stages of shifting comparative advantage" model is that both Korea and Taiwan found themselves in the second stage, the one in which manufactured exports rely heavily on material- and resource-based products. From the mid-1960s through the next 10 to 15 years, they were both entering the third stage, in which exports tend to be labor-intensive simple consumer goods. It was only in the 1980s that both countries were clearly entering the fourth stage, in which the emphasis shifts away from consumer to machinery and other sophisticated products.

When studying the NICs' exports decomposed by markets, a wide divergence in the embodied consumer goods ratio is found. In 1965, the beginning of the serious export-led development drive of the NICs, 70% of NIC exports to the EC were consumer goods. The comparable ratios for the U.S. and Japanese markets were 58% and 46%, respectively. One way to make sense of this divergence and of observed developments by market over time is to posit that at the start of the period (the early 1960s), the NICs were in Stage 2 (raw material and early material-based exports) vis-à-vis the Japanese market. With respect to the European and the U.S. markets, however, they were already in Stage 3. The reason the Japanese market differed in the opportunities it offered the NICs is that Japan's trade pattern was such that it ran a large surplus in manufactures and a large deficit in fuels and raw materials. In addition, the Pacific Basin (including the NICs) was the "natural" region from which Japan tended to import raw materials (similarly, Latin America

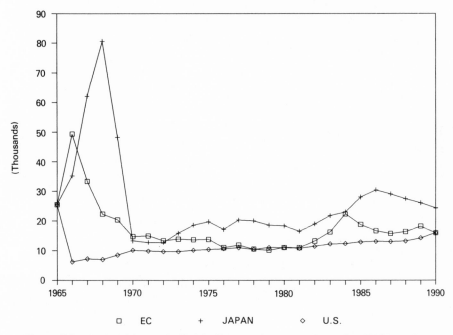

Figure 5.7   Capital/labor embodied in Singapore's exports, by major OECD market.

played this role for the United States and African and other former colonies did so for the EC).

If this interpretation is correct, one could expect to find that as the NICs developed more industrial sophistication, they would tend to move on to Stage 3 in the Japanese market then to Stage 4 in the other two OECD markets. Figures 5.13 presents the NIC average consumer goods ratios by major OECD markets. The patterns observed in Figure 5.13 suggest that the NICs moved through their stages of dynamic comparative advantage at different rates in the respective markets. During the rapid-growth period of 1965 to the mid-1970s, the proportion of consumer goods in NIC exports to Japan expanded rapidly, reaching a high of 57% of these exports in 1978. As argued previously, this dramatic shift represented a shift in the comparative advantage of the NICs as they gained sophistication in their production process (moving from Stage 2 to Stage 3).[8] On the demand side, of course, this also represented the tendency of Japan to shift its sources of raw materials and materials-based (e.g., rubber or simple textile) products to lower cost ASEAN countries.

However, from the late 1970s on, this shift ended, and a clear decline took place in the proportion of consumer goods in the Japan-destined exports. This indicates the rapidity with which the NICs went through the trade-development stages. By the late 1970s and 1980s, the NICs were clearly shifting from Stage 3 to Stage 4 in the Japanese market as their exports became increasingly less typified by simple labor-intensive consumer goods. By 1987 only 45% of the NIC exports to Japan were

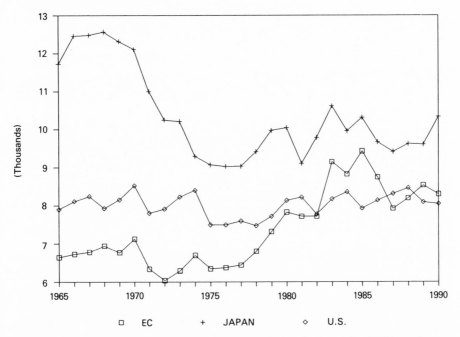

Figure 5.8 Capital/labor embodied in Hong Kong's exports, by major OECD market.

classified as consumer goods. By 1990 a clear convergence in the three OECD (sub)markets is observed with respect to the consumer ratio. This may reflect a maturation of the NICs' economies: by the early 1990s the NICs had been increasingly focusing their exports to all OECD markets in terms of relatively sophisticated nonconsumer products.

In both the United States and (especially) the EC, the NICs were already solidly in Stage 3 in the mid-1960s. And, as expected, the subsequent period saw a steady movement to Stage 4 in these two markets. In both, the proportion of consumer goods clearly declined as a proportion of the total NIC exports in each market. By the late 1980s the proportion was under 50% in each of these markets, having begun as 58% and 70% of the U.S. and EC markets in the mid-1960s. In 1990 the proportion of consumer goods in the NICs' exports to the United States and the EC were, respectively, 45% and 49%.

TWO MEASURES OF HUMAN CAPITAL:
WAGE PER WORKER AND THE SKILL RATIO

The trends just noted are repeated when one examines two measures of human capital, the skill ratio (SR) and wage per worker.[9] In both cases there is indicated a clear increase in embodied human capital (i.e., a continuous shift to products embodying a higher proportion of human capital) over the full two and a half

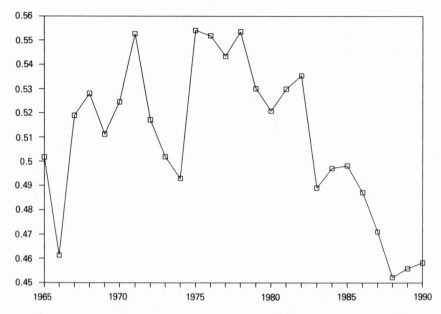

Figure 5.9 Consumer goods proportion of Korea's exports, by OECD market.

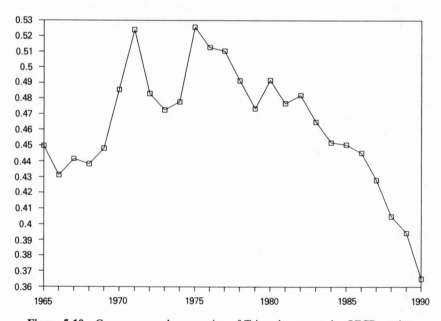

Figure 5.10 Consumer goods proportion of Taiwan's exports, by OECD market.

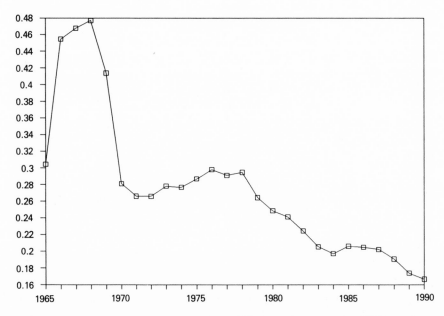

Figure 5.11 Consumer goods proportion of Singapore's exports, by OECD market.

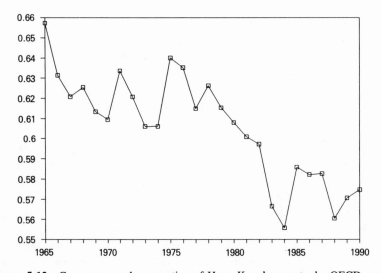

Figure 5.12 Consumer goods proportion of Hong Kong's exports, by OECD market.

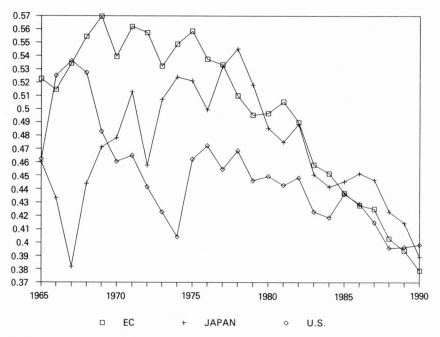

Figure 5.13   Consumer goods proportion of NIC exports, by OECD market.

decades examined in NIC exports to the United States and to the EC. The same is true for Japan-bound exports from the NICs after the mid-1970s. In the case of these two measures of human capital (unlike the case of the physical capital/labor ratio), a convergence to a growing similarity between the three markets is evident by the late 1980s.

As measured by these two indicators, the NICs ranked by embodied human capital are Singapore, followed by Taiwan, Korea, and finally, Hong Kong. Figures 5.14 through 5.19 present the two human-capital measures by NIC and by market.

PRODUCT CYCLE THEORY: EVIDENCE OF SHIFTING TO STAGE 5—R&D-INTENSIVE EXPORTS

The fifth stage describes a situation in which the country's comparative advantage comes increasingly to be based on technology-gap (product-cycle) factors; this stage was found by Kellman and Landau to characterize Japan's situation by the early 1980s. Support for this hypothesis includes a growing degree of product differentiation associated with the respective export vectors, since as one moves from reliance on homogeneous "mature" products to innovative, state-of-the-art, product-cycle products, one expects less standardization to characterize the relevant exports. The product differentiation index (PR) calculated for the three export vectors is graphed in Figure 5.20.[10]

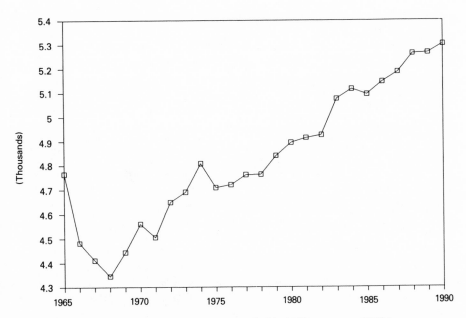

Figure 5.14 Wage per worker embodied in NIC exports to OECD.

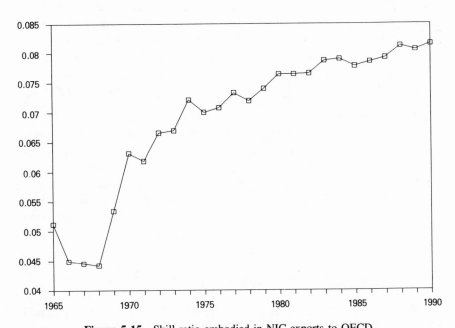

Figure 5.15 Skill ratio embodied in NIC exports to OECD.

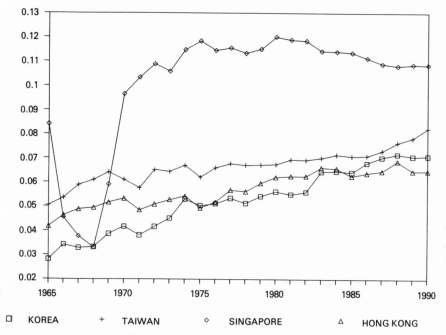

Figure 5.16   Skill ratio embodied in NIC exports to OECD, by NIC.

Figure 5.20 shows a clear increase over the entire period in this proxy for product sophistication for products shipped to the EC and for the first decade (1965–75) for those shipped to the United States; however, little if any systematic change is evident for Japan-bound NIC exports. The index increased till 1982, then showed a clear decline to 1990. In the U.S. market, the product differentiation measure tended to decline somewhat after 1977. Thus while this measure would indicate a fairly continuous shift toward a more sophisticated export pattern throughout the two decades examined here from the NICs to the EC market, it does not support the hypothesized shift to Stage 5 in the U.S. and Japanese markets in the 1980s.

A different indicator of product sophistication—the "first-trade date" (FS)—yields better consistent support for this hypothesis.[11] As a country's exports shift to a higher composition of "newer" or more sophisticated product-cycle products, one would expect the average date to gradually increase. Studying Figure 5.21, we find a clear upward trend to have taken hold only in the 1980s. The first-trade index tends upward in the U.S. and EC markets after 1980 and in the Japanese market after 1986.

RESULTS OF STEPWISE REGRESSION

Several sets of export vectors for selected years (1965, 1970, 1975, 1980, and 1987, with 101 observations each) for each NIC–market combination were regressed against the six product characteristics developed by Hufbauer discussed in this

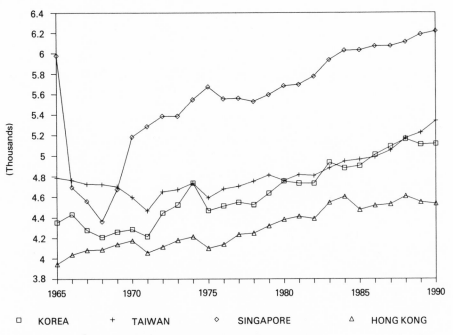

Figure 5.17 Wage per worker, by NIC.

chapter. These were exploratory regressions, intended to uncover those characteristics and combinations of characteristics that had statistically significant explanatory power. The SAS stepwise procedure was used (with the max_r option, which
determines the best 1-, 2-, . . . , n-variable models). Table 5.1 lists the variables
that were selected as significant determinants, or explainers, of the export product
compositions for each of the respective years. The implication is that if a variable
does not appear in the table, it was "selected out" that is, it was not a significant
embodied characteristic of the respective export vector.

From Table 5.1 it is evident that the only characteristic which clearly and consistently distinguished both South Korea's and Hong Kong's exports in all three OECD
markets was low wages. The only market–period cell in which any other characteristic played a role in defining or describing the factors underlying Korea's exports
to Japan was in 1975 when, in addition to low wages, the first-trade characteristic
became somewhat significant (at 10%). This indicates that toward the mid-1970s,
immediately following the first world oil crisis, South Korea began to export to
Japan products whose product-life-cycle designation tended to be less "mature" and
standardized, and more innovative, closer to the cutting edge of technology. This
tendency, however, was no longer evident in the 1980s or 1990s.

The same single factor—low wages—characterized Hong Kong's export success
in all three OECD markets throughout the period studied. The only exception was in
Hong Kong's exports to Japan in 1980, when the consumer goods ratio joined low
wages as a significant identifiable factor.

Taiwan's profile is quite different from those of South Korea and Hong Kong.

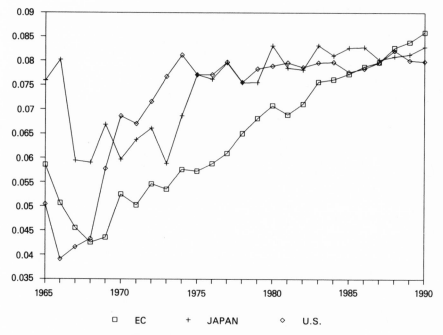

Figure 5.18   Skill ratio, by market.

While low wages here, too, formed an important basis for export success in all three markets throughout the entire period examined—as evidenced by the appearance of the wages variable in each market–period cell—other embodied characteristics played important roles as well. In the mid-1960s, the first-trade date appeared as a significant explainer of Taiwan exports to the EC and to Japan and as a somewhat less significant explainer of exports to the United States. As noted in the previous paragraph, this suggests that Taiwan's exports had a bias in favor of "newer," more technologically innovative products at that time.

Another characteristic unique to Taiwan's exports is the appearance of the capital/labor ratio (KL) with a significantly positive coefficient in its exports both to the EC and to Japan in the mid-1960s. Indeed, an examination of Figure 5.2 indicates that Taiwan's exports to these two markets did indeed embody a relatively capital-intensive product mix, one which declined sharply through the late 1960s to mid-1970s, when it began to rise again, though only slightly. It is notable that the KL characteristic does not appear again in any later period in any of Taiwan's (OECD) export markets except in Japan-bound exports in 1990, when the KL embodiment enters with a significantly negative coefficient. This could be taken as evidence of a correctly operating market, which, as it was freed from official controls, focused increasingly on products wherein lay Taiwan's comparative advantage. These were certainly not in capital-intensive industries during the period studied here.

Finally, Singapore demonstrates a unique pattern of underlying export charac-

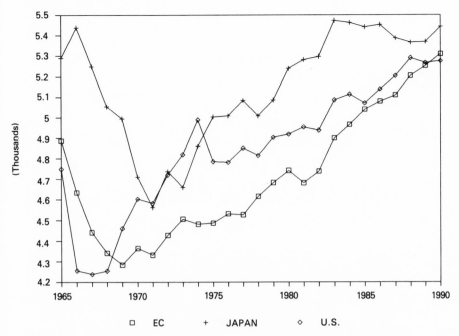

Figure 5.19 Wage per worker, by market.

teristics. Of all the NICs, it is here alone that the wages characteristic played a minor role. It appears significant in relatively few cases, during the earlier period. In 1970 the wage variable was only of marginal significance (10%) for its exports to the United States. From the mid-1970s low wages played no significant role in defining and explaining Singapore's export drive to any of the three markets. Instead, the variable "skill" (skilled labor ratio) appears ubiquitously throughout all three markets. This indicates that Singapore increasingly found its comparative advantage on a higher technological plateau, based on highly skilled human capital. It may be noted that a comparative advantage based on human capital is typically found to underlie the comparative advantage of the United States and Japan. Other characteristics, such as product differentiation measure and first-trade date, which also appear as definers and explainers of Singapore's export success in the late 1970s and early 1990s, support the contention that Singapore had moved to a Stage 5 level of export sophistication well ahead of the other NICs.

SUMMARY

An examination of compositional shifts in NIC exports to the major OECD markets—not in terms of products, but rather in terms of embodied factors and characteristics—supports the hypothesis that the past several decades may be understood in terms of a clear linear "maturation" process. The NIC export patterns followed

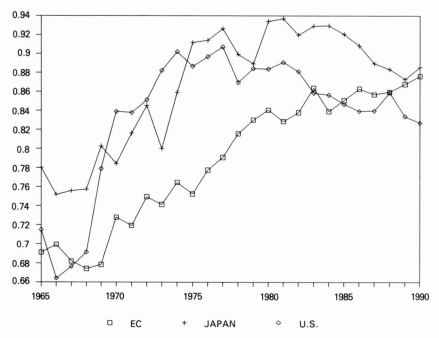

Figure 5.20   Product differentiation index, by market.

the five-stage process suggested by Balassa and others. In this dynamic process, Singapore and then Taiwan may be seen as leading while Hong Kong is lagging.

In terms of different OECD markets, each tended to play a different role in the process. Thus during the middle and late 1960s—the start of our sample period—NIC exports to both the EC and the United States exhibited a clear decrease in the proportion of consumer goods, characteristic of the fourth stage. A shift to this stage in the Japanese market was not evident until the early 1980s. In terms of the embodied capital/labor ratios, the NICs' export patterns matched expectations generated by a simple Ricardian or Heckscher–Ohlin factor-proportions model until the mid-1970s. However, from this date to the early 1990s a clear increase in the capital/labor intensity describes NIC exports to each of the three markets. This finding is consistent with our interpretation of the consumer goods proportion: by the late 1970s, the NICs were moving through a more sophisticated Stage 4 in their development process—moving away from simple labor-intensive consumer goods— and finding their comparative advantage in more sophisticated capital-intensive production.

In terms of technological maturity indicators, such as measures of product differentiation or measures of embodied human capital, the U.S. market tended to play a lesser role, absorbing exports differentiated mainly, and often exclusively, by the relatively low wage embodied in their production. On the other hand, the Japanese market tended to absorb more sophisticated export mixes during the past decade. An interesting finding is that during the mid-1970s, when Singapore and Taiwan and, to

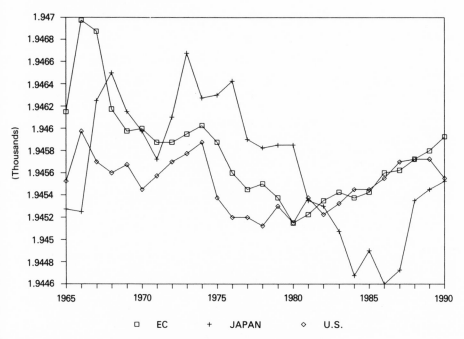

Figure 5.21 First-trade date, by market.

a lesser extent, the others, were moving into the fifth stage, they also tended to focus on increasingly capital-intensive (higher capital/labor ratios) products, indicating that the new technologies were typically embodied in new investment goods.

NOTES

1. The product characteristics, such as capital/labor ratios, utilized in these and the following diagrams pertain to one year. Thus the neoclassic assumption of invariant technology is maintained and the observed changes may be unequivocally interpreted in terms of relative export specialization shifts.

2. Balassa (1979).

3. For a summary of this theory and an application to Japan, see Kellman and Landau (1984).

4. The general argument is that once sufficient liberalization allowed market prices to determine relative profitabilities, this led to an expansion of labor-intensive industries in each of the NICs.

5. The capital/labor ratios of the four NICs were low relative to exports of other comparable countries—notably the Latin American NICs. See Kellman and Carney (1981), table III.5, p. 113.

6. Bradford and Branson (1987), p. 28.

7. This complementary pattern between Japan's economy and the NICs' and ASEAN economies was noted by Yamazawa (1987).

8. The hypothesis is given independent support by Chow's (1990) finding of a shrinking revealed comparative advantage index over time for these same countries.

9. The skill ratio is the percentage of the industry's labor force accounted for in the United States in 1960 by professionals and technical and scientific personnel. See Hufbauer (1970).

10. The PR index was calculated as the coefficient of variation in seven-digit Schedule B products

Table 5.1   Export Embodied Characteristics
from Stepwise Regressions for Selected Years

	South Korea	Taiwan	Singapore	Hong Kong
	Exports to the United States			
1965	Wage	Wage FID*	NA	Wage
1970	Wage	Wage	Wage* PRD*	Wage
1975	Wage	Wage	PRD	Wage
1980	Wage	Wage	Skill KL*	Wage
1990	Wage	Wage	—	Wage
	Exports to EC			
1965	Wage	Wage KL CG FID	NA	Wage
1970	Wage	Wage FID	Wage	Wage
1975	Wage	Wage	KL* FID*	Wage
1980	Wage	Wage	KL Skill*	Wage
1990	Wage	(−)KL	—	Wage
	Exports to Japan			
1965	Wage	KL CG	NA	Wage
1970	Wage	Wage FID	Wage	Wage
1975	Wage FID*	Wage	Skill CG	Wage
1980	Wage	Wage FID*	Skill CG* PRD*	Wage CG
1990	Wage	Wage FID*	Skill	Wage

Note: Asterisks indicate variables significant at 90% level. All others are at
95% level of significance. CG = consumer goods ratio; FID = first-trade
date; KL = capital/labor ratio; PRD = product differentiation index; Skill =
skilled labor ratio. In all cases in which wages were significant, the coefficient is preceded by a negative sign.

within four-digit product groups' unit values of 1965 U.S. exports destined to different countries.
Differentiated products are marked by higher coefficients of variation.

11. The first-trade date is defined as the date at which this product initially appeared in U.S. import
data in substantial quantity. See Hufbauer (1970).

REFERENCES

Balassa, Bela. 1979. "The Changing Pattern of Comparative Advantage in Manufactured Goods."
   Review of Economics and Statistics 61:259–66.

————. 1981. *The Newly Industrializing Countries in the World Economy.* New York: Pergamon Press.

Bradford, C., and W. Branson (eds.). 1987. *Trade and Structural Change in Pacific Asia.* Chicago: University of Chicago Press.

Chow, Peter C. Y.. 1990. "The Revealed Comparative Advantage of the East Asian NICs." *International Trade Journal* 5, no. 2:235–62.

Hanink, Dean M. 1990. "Linder, Again." *Weltwirtschaftliches Archiv* 126, no. 2:257–67.

Hufbauer, G. 1970. "The Impact of National Characteristics and Technology on the Commodity Composition of Trade in Manufactured Goods." In R. Vernon (ed.), *The Technology Factor in International Trade.* New York: National Bureau of Economic Research, pp. 145–232.

Kellman, M., and R. Carney. 1981. Comparison and Summary of the Characteristics of NIC Exports to the Western Industrialized Economies. Lexington, MA: Data Resources, Inc.

Kellman, Mitchell, and D. Landau. 1984. "The Nature of Japan's Comparative Advantage, 1965–80." *World Development* 12, no. 4:433–38.

Khana, Ashok. 1985. "A Note on the Dynamic Aspects of the Hechscher–Ohlin Model: Some Empirical Evidence." *World Development* 13, nos. 10–11:1171–74.

Krugman, Paul. 1983. "New Theories of Trade Among Industrial Countries." *American Economic Review* 73:343–47.

Linder, S. B. 1961. *An Essay on Trade and Transformation.* New York: Wiley.

McKinnon, R. I. 1982. "Currency Substitution and Instability in the World Dollar Standard." *American Economic Review* 72, no. 3:320–33.

————. 1984. *An International Standard for Monetary Stabilization.* Washington, D.C.: Institute for International Economics.

Vernon, R. 1979. "The Product Cycle Hypothesis in a New International Environment." *Oxford Bulletin of Economics and Statistics* 41:255–67.

Yamazawa, I. 1987. "Japan and Her Asian Neighbors in a Dynamic Perspective." In C. Bradford and W. Branson (eds.), *Trade and Structural Change in Pacific Asia.* Chicago: University of Chicago press, pp. 93–119.

6

Coping with OECD Protectionism

Trade barriers facing NICs' manufactured exports exceed those facing industrialized countries. This fairly noncontroversial, generally accepted statement may be said to enjoy the status of today's conventional wisdom (e.g., see Markusen). A perusal of the literature finds that economists tend to concur with the observation that OECD tariff structures are systematically biased against LDC exports (e.g., see Helleiner, Meier, and UNCTAD), and that, subsequently, LDCs have always viewed the GATT as being antagonistic to their interests.

The successive GATT rounds, and in particular the Kennedy round (1964–67), demonstrably lowered tariff and protection levels across the board, and this clearly applied to products exported by developing countries as well (e.g., see Preeg). Nevertheless, it is generally contended that the discrimination suffered by the developing countries remained constant, if not actually increasing through the recent GATT rounds (Ray, 1987; Ray and Marvel, 1984).

However, the reason for this "revealed discrimination" is not clear. A reading of the development and trade literature suggests various hypotheses. One argument holds that this is the cumulative result of a "neo-imperialistic" process through which the industrialized "center" tends to systematically exploit its monopsonistic position, in the context of the dynamic tendency of the developing "periphery" to specialize in products whose (price) supply elasticity is low.

Another hypothesis is that the anti-LDC discrimination is the inadvertent cumulative effect of an uneven bargaining process. Since most products traditionally of interest to LDC exporters were not heavily represented in trade to industrialized countries, they tended to be systematically excluded from most favored nation (MFN) agreements.

Studies by Ray and Marvel and Ray (1984) explicitly view the GATT rounds as opportunities for special interests in the industrialized countries to reregulate (rather than deregulate) and reestablish historic protection for declining industries, primarily consumer goods and textiles. Thus the growing measures of protectionism are attributed to conscious design on the part of the GATT negotiators, whose focus is on product characteristics (e.g., labor intensity). The fact that these products are of paramount interest to emerging LDC exporters of manufactured products is only incidental.

In stark contrast, Verreydt and Waelbroeck's noted study focused on the source of these manufactures rather than their characteristics. They emphasized the inability of developing countries (DCs) to effectively retaliate against discriminatory protectionist policies of the EC.

Though differing from one another in many ways, all these explanations agree that the observed NIC–DC tariff differentials are attributable to actions taken by the industrialized DCs. In point of fact, it is rather difficult to determine the extent to which observed protection differentials may be laid at the doorstep of the behavior, conscious or otherwise, of the industrialized countries. No systematic empirical or econometric work has been done in this area. It is the purpose of this chapter to examine the validity of this general proposition.

There is no question that two recent (Kennedy and Tokyo) GATT rounds have resulted in significantly lower tariffs. For our sample of 269 manufactured products the average rate of protection fell from 15% in the pre-Kennedy period (1964) to 5% in the post-Tokyo era (1979).[1] Despite these drastic cuts, however, the relative tariff structure remained rather fixed. The Pearson correlation coefficient between the (trade-weighted) average 1964 tariffs and 1979 tariff was 0.695.[2]

In light of this relative structural fixity, the following finding is perhaps unexpected: whereas the pre-Kennedy round tariffs were found not to discriminate significantly against NIC-sourced products, the post-Tokyo round tariffs clearly did. Table 6.1 summarizes the relevant statistics. These were obtained from a bivariate regression of the trade-weighted average tariffs on the NIC shares of U.S.-manufactured imports in 1964 and 1979.

The results summarized in Table 6.1 strongly suggest that the skepticism with which the NICs view the results of the two most recent GATT rounds seems amply justified. No statistically significant relationship existed between the relative nominal tariff levels and the relative importance of NIC suppliers in the mid-1960s—the period preceding the Kennedy round. Those products in which NICs were relatively predominant were not subject to above-average tariffs. However, the corresponding *t* statistics for the late post-Tokyo round (1970s) was a clearly positive and significant 5.825. That is, by the late 1970s those manufactured products of which the NICs held relatively large shares of the U.S. import market clearly encountered higher than average tariff levels.

The picture one gets is that of a protectionist United States and, by extension, other OECD countries,[3] actively and purposefully fine-tuning their protection structures to more effectively exclude products sourced in the NICs.[4]

Table 6.1 *t* Values from Regression Coefficients of Tariff Levels on NIC Market Share Measures, Selected Years

NIC Share of U.S. Imports	Trade-Weighted Average	
	1964	1979
1966	−0.239	0.649
1977	3.899	5.825

However, a closer examination of the results summarized in Table 6.1 casts a strong doubt on this particular interpretation. No significant discrimination against NICs' exports was found in the pre-Kennedy round period, nor did the post-Tokyo round tariff structure discriminate against NICs' 1966 export composition. If the intent of the GATT conferees had indeed been to discriminate against NIC-sourced products, presumably they would have levied relatively high tariffs against those products in which NICs dominated the OECD import market at the start of the bargaining rounds. In fact, what appears to have happened is that during the period of these two rounds (early 1960s to late 1970s) the NICs gained shares in the U.S. import market primarily in nontraditional manufactured products. In our sample, the Pearson correlation between the NICs' share of U.S. manufactured imports in 1960 and the change in shares from 1966 to 1977 is -0.83. Both the pre-Kennedy and the post-Tokyo rounds levied significantly higher tariffs against those products in which NICs demonstrated revealed competitiveness in the late 1970s but not against those products in which NICs were especially visible at the start of the Kennedy round.

PRODUCT CHARACTERISTICS VERSUS
GEOGRAPHIC ORIGINATION

Lavergne notes that studies to date have failed to separate the influences of the actual sourcing of imports in NICs from the nature of the products themselves.[5] It may be that the tariff discriminates against NIC-sourced producers not per se but rather because such products happen to incorporate, or embody, heavily tariffed characteristics. As suggested by Lavergne, this issue may be fruitfully analyzed in the context of a multivariate regression model.

While much professional and official concern has been expressed concerning the plight of the NICs, it has been very difficult to clearly identify the exact nature of the protectionist discrimination they face. This is because such a demonstration would have to sort out the effects of the nature of the products that tend to be sourced in the NICs from the actual fact of their being sourced there. Though it may appear obvious to some that the actual sourcing is of no significance (it is generally accepted that tariffs and NTBs are levied on products, not on countries), such reasoning is out of touch with typical perceptions in NIC (and UNCTAD) circles. The very existence of countervailing tariffs and voluntary export restraints (VERs) proves that the protectionist process is not "source blind." Deductive logic indicates that the producers of import substitutes should not care where the imports come from as long as the total value or volume of imports is limited, but in fact protection schemes are often designed to affect trade flows on a conscious geographic basis. As indicated previously, Lavergne concluded that it is precisely the failure to distinguish between product characteristics and country sourcing that constitutes an important weakness in current research in this area. We undertake this research task in the following section.

THE REGRESSION MODEL

Much work has been done in developing models to "explain" tariff levels as functions of comparative disadvantage, pressure group action, transition costs to governments, and other factors. Seminal works in this area include Anderson (1987), Caves (1976), Fieleke (1976), Finger and DeRosa (1978), Pincus (1975), Ray (1981), Saunders (1979), and Travis (1964). We rely here on a composite which embodies the accepted and rather conventional specifications found to explain tariff structures in these works. Our model is

$$T_i = f(\text{NIC}, E_{76}, \text{MOFA}, \text{EVA}, \text{RND}, \text{SPEC}, T_{30}, \text{TEXT}, \text{CONS})$$

where

T_i	= average weighted tariff level for good i
E_{76}	= total employment in 1976
MOFA	= proportion of U.S. imports originating from majority-owned affiliates of U.S. corporations
EVA	= labor cost in each dollar of imports (labor intensity)
RND	= scientists and engineers as a percentage of total employment (R&D-embodied labor)
SPEC	= proportion of all revenue represented by specific (as compared to ad valorem) tariffs
T_{30}	= weighted average tariff level in 1930
TEXT	= dummy variable which takes the value of 1 for textiles
CONS	= dummy variable which takes the value of 1 for consumer goods

In this formula NIC takes on various specifications: the proportion of all imports originating in NICs (in 1966); the change in the NIC share of all U.S. imports from 1966 to 1977; the rate of change of NIC exports to the United States from 1966 to 1977.

A detailed theoretical discussion of this and of alternative specifications may be found in Lavergne (1983), whose notation we adopt here. The original data sources are also discussed in Lavergne.

Table 6.2 summarizes the t statistics for this model. The results are as expected. The explanatory power of the model is fairly good—from one-half to two-thirds of the variation in the nominal tariff rates is explained. As expected, the tariff rates are strongly (and positively) associated with the relative rankings of the infamous Smoot–Hawley tariff. Generally the historical pattern of tariffs is maintained through the post-Kennedy and Tokyo periods.[6]

The R&D variable was a big surprising. Instead of the negative coefficient one would have expected to find in this measure of relative U.S. strength, one finds a significantly positive sign in the 1964 tariff structure. This may perhaps be explained in terms of national security considerations. In any case, from 1972 the coefficient is no longer significant, indicating that the Kennedy round cuts tended to "rationalize" this dimension of the protection structure.

Table 6.2   *t* Statistics of Full Sample Model
($N = 269$)

Independent Variable	Trade-Weighted Average		
	1964	1972	1979
T_{30}	16.5	13.4	6.9
RND	2.7	1.6	1.0
EVA	4.8	5.6	3.4
MOFA	−1.0	−1.5	−1.9
SPEC	−4.2	−2.2	−4.5
E	−2.3	−0.9	+1.2
TEXT	1.70	3.0	5.2
CONS	0.4	1.4	2.9
R^2	0.66	0.64	0.50

The variable indicating the relative importance of U.S. multinational corporations does have the expected negative sign. However, it becomes statistically significant only in the post–Tokyo round period, perhaps indicating this particular economic institution's growing political clout during the 1970s and into the 1980s.

SPEC, measuring the relative weight of revenue originating from specific tariffs (in 1964), plays its expected role. Clearly, Congress does not systematically update tariffs to compensate for inflationary erosion.

E, the scale measure, does have the expected neg ve coefficient in the pre-Kennedy round period. However, from 1972 on this is no longer the case. There are many possible explanations for this. Mancur Olson, for example, argued that the very size of an industry made it harder to organize (for political leverage) rapidly enough to protect against relative erosion during the rather drastic tariff cuts that characterized the Kennedy round period of 1964–1969.

Table 6.3 indicates the *t* values obtained for the NICs' export-sourcing variables when "embedded" into the regression model. In this way, the "NIC origination factor" is accounted for, having taken into account the relevant product characteristics.

When comparing these results to those summarized in Table 6.1, especially the lower right portions of the respective tables, it becomes clear that the NIC-source variables have no independent explanatory power in the context of the full model. Products have higher than average nominal tariffs because they have always (at least

Table 6.3   *t* Values of Regression Coefficients of NIC Origination Variables and Nominal Tariff Levels from Multivariate Model

NIC Origination Factor	Trade-Weighted Average		
	1964	1972	1979
1966	0.12	0.30	0.90
1966–77	0.51	0.08	−0.14
1977	1.36	0.79	1.54

Table 6.4 Product Characteristics by Sample Classified by NIC Shares of U.S. Import Market

Variables/Samples	NIC 1966 Share		NIC 1977 Share	
	Greater than 10%	Less than 10%	Greater than 20%	Less than 20%
E	795	1,482	1,217	1,550
SPEC	0.16	0.14	0.19	0.10
MOFA	0.16	0.12	0.08	0.16
RND	0.03	0.03	0.02	0.04
EVA	1.17	1.12	1.29	0.97
TEXT	0.21	0.15	0.26	0.06
CONS	0.23	0.27	0.38	0.17
	t Statistics (t test)			
	1966		1977	
E	1.94		2.30	
SPEC	0.16		2.56	
MOFA	1.07		4.43	
EVA	0.52		7.06	
TEXT	0.66		4.94	
CONS	0.39		5.56	

since the 1930s) been highly tariffed, or because they are labor intensive, or they embody this or another characteristic which for various reasons discussed earlier tend to elicit high tariff protection in the United States. Once these characteristics have been explicitly taken into account, the fact that these products happen to originate in NICs has no further effect.

If indeed the product characteristics were the "true" explanatory variables of the distinctly higher tariffs found to apply to NIC-"dominated" products, one would expect to find significant discrimination for these variables in the pre-Kennedy round era (1964), since it was found that no significant tariff differentials applied to that period. The results appear in Table 6.4.

The results are dramatic. With the single possible exception of employment, the relative share of NICs in U.S. imports for the 1966 period did not discriminate successfully for any of the explanatory variables. However, for the post-Tokyo round period, the two samples were significantly and consistently differentiated from one another in terms of each of the variables, with the sole exceptions of 1930 tariff levels.

SUMMARY

An examination of a large sample of 269 manufactured products imported into the U.S. market during the periods immediately preceding and following the Kennedy and Tokyo rounds yields a fairly unequivocable answer to the question of whether the recent GATT rounds were discriminatory against the NICs. At the conclusion of the most recent Tokyo round, the average nominal tariff rates were clearly higher for products in which NICs held a relatively higher share in the U.S. import market. In this respect, one can clearly conclude that the GATT process does indeed lead to anti-NIC bias, thus justifying its "rich man's club" reputation in the Third World.

However, a careful examination of the time sequences indicates that between the mid-1960s and the late 1970s the NICs vigorously and rapidly expanded their overall presence in the manufactured-import market of the United States, precisely in those product groups already subject to relatively high tariffs. In other words, rather than the U.S. tariff structure deliberately "knocking out" the newly emerging competitive stance of the NICs in manufactures, the NIC export drive "walked right into the right hook."

In particular, it was found that during this period NICs expanded especially in product categories that had traditionally (since 1930) been highly tariffed, in products that were highly labor intensive, in products that were less categorized by specific tariff, in products that were less likely to be produced by U.S.-owned multinational corporations (relative to non-NIC-sourced products), and especially in products that fell under the overall categories of textiles or consumer goods—two areas especially sensitive to protectionist sentiment in the United States.

These results may be explained in terms of the systematic process of dynamic diffusion of comparative advantage as presented by Balassa, Kellman and Yun, and others. Those industries in which the NICs tend to find their comparative advantage are precisely the industries characterized by low skills and slow growth in the industrial countries, where comparative advantage tends to shift to other industries and sectors. As noted by Bhagwati (1982a), these declining industries are particularly likely targets of lobbying pressure for protection.

NOTES

This chapter draws largely on M. H. Kellman and P. C. Y. Chow, "Anti-LDC Bias in the U.S. Tariff Structure: A Test of Source versus Product Characteristics," *Review of Economics and Statistics* 70, no. 4 (November 1988):648–53.

1. The data used this study—a sample of 269 manufactured products—were provided by Real Lavergne. The data and variables used are described in detail in Lavergne (1983).

2. The fact that in spite of rather drastic nominal tariff cuts, the pattern of protection remained relatively unchanged has been noted in the literature (e.g., Lavergne, 1983; Ray and Marvel, 1984).

3. Preeg (1970) noted that the concessions granted the NICs by the United States during the Kennedy round were similar to those granted by other large industrial countries.

4. A comparable literature, going back to Walter (1971), demonstrates a disproportionately frequent application of nontariff barriers (NTBs) to NIC exports. Several studies have established a positive relationship between tariff rates and NTBs (e.g., Ray, 1981; Ray and Marvel, 1984). Hence the results of our study may be generalized to apply to tariff and NTB protection patterns. In any case, NTBs were of little importance for manufactures other than textiles and clothing (Little, 1982, p. 292).

5. See Lavergne (1983), p. 120.

6. See Ray and Marvel (1984), p. 454.

REFERENCES

Anderson, K. 1987. "The Political Market for Government Assistance to Industries." Paper presented to the seventh conference of economists at Macquarie University, Sydney, Australia, August.

Balassa, Bela. 1981. *The Newly Industrializing Countries in the World Economy.* New York: Pergamon Press, pp. 147–67.

Bhagwati, J. 1982a. "Shifting Comparative Advantage, Protectionist Demand, and Policy Response." In *Import Competition and Response.* Chicago: National Bureau of Economic Research. pp. 153–84.

———— (ed.). 1982b. *Import Competition and Responses.* Chicago: National Bureau of Economic Research.

Caves, R.. 1976. "Economic Models of Political Choice: Canada's Tariff Structure." *Canadian Journal of Economics* 9, no. 2 (May):278–300.

Congressional Budget Office. 1987. *The GATT Negotiations and U.S. Trade Policy.* Washington, D.C.: USGPO, pp. 29–30.

Fieleke, N.. 1976. "The Tariff Structure for Manufacturing Industries in the United States: A Test of Some Traditional Explanations." *Columbia Journal of World Business* 12 (Winter):98–104.

Finger, M., and D. DeRosa. 1978. "Trade Overlap, Comparative Advantage and Protection." In Herbert Giersh (ed.), *On the Economics of Intra-Industry Trade: Symposium.* Tübingen: Mohr, pp. 213–40.

Helleiner, G. 1977. "The Political Economy of Canada's Tariff Structure: An Alternative Model." *Canadian Journal of Economics* 10, no. 2 (May):318–26.

Kellman, M., and Y. Yun. 1983. "Korea—Tomorrow's Japan." *Journal of Economic Development* 10:125–38.

Lavergne, R. 1983. *The Political Economy of U.S. Tariffs—An Empirical Study.* New York: Academic Press.

Little, I. 1982. *Economic Development.* New York: Basic Books.

Markusen, J. 1986. "Explaining the Volume of Trade: An Eclectic Approach." *American Economic Review* 76, no. 5 (December):1002–11.

Meier, G. 1984. *Leading Issues in Economic Development,* 4th ed. New York: Oxford University Press, 1984.

Pincus, J. 1975. "Pressure Groups and the Pattern of Tariffs." *Journal of Political Economy* 83, no. 4 (August):757–78.

Preeg, E. 1970. *Traders and Diplomats.* Washington, D.C.: The Brookings Institution.

Ray, E. 1981. "The Determinants of Tariff and Non-Tariff Trade Restrictions in the United States." *Journal of Political Economy* 89, no. 1 (February):105–21.

————. 1987. "The Impact of Special Interests on Preferential Tariff Concessions by the United States." *Review of Economics and Statistics* 69 (May):187–93.

Ray, E., and H. Marvel. 1984. "The Pattern of Protection in the Industrial World." *Review of Economics and Statistics* 66 (August):452–58.

Saunders, R.. 1979. "The Political Economy of Effective Tariff Protection in Canada's Manufacturing Sector." *Canadian Journal of Economics* 12:38–44.

Travis, W. 1964. *The Theory of Trade and Protection.* Cambridge, Mass.: Harvard University Press.

UNCTAD. 1967. *The Question of Granting Extension of Preferences in Favor of Developing Countries.* Geneva: UNCTAD.

Verreydt, E., and J. Waelbroeck. 1982. "European Community Protection Against Manufactured Imports from Developing Countries: A Case Study in Political Economy of Protection." In J. Bhagwati (ed.), *Import Competition and Response.* Chicago: National Bureau of Economic Research, 1982.

Walter, I. 1971. "Non-Tariff Barriers and the Export Performance of Developing Countries." *American Economic Review* 61 (May):195–205.

7

Balancing Imports and Exports with OECD

During the past quarter century, the NICs have expanded their manufactures export share of the OECD import markets roughly threefold, from 1.7% in 1965 to about 5% in 1990. What is less well appreciated is that their import market also expanded continuously over this period. By expanding their import markets, the NICs provide potential outlets for other NICs' exports and potential solutions to imbalances in trade flows in the Pacific region trade.

Tables 7.1 through 7.4 document the growth of OECD-sourced imports into each of the four NICs from 1965 to 1990. It is clear that all four NICs' import markets grew rapidly for exports of all three major regions of the OECD. U.S.-manufactured exports grew at an average (compounded) rate of roughly 20% per year through the 1965–90 period to Taiwan and Korea, 24.6% to Singapore, and "only" 15% to Hong Kong. In 1990 the United States exported $8.6 billion of manufactured products to Korea, $7.7 billion to Taiwan, $6.7 billion to Singapore, and $4.1 billion to Hong Kong. All four imported somewhat more from Japan in 1990 and, with the exception of Hong Kong, somewhat less from the EC. From Tables 7.1 through 7.4 it is clear that the impressive increases in OECD-sourced imports into the NICs were broadly based, shared by most of the 13 manufactured categories.

In this chapter we examine the relationships between the NICs' exports and their corresponding imports. In general, a country's exports and imports are related in two ways. The first is by a simple budget constraint. In order to import, a country must obtain foreign exchange or foreign credit. In the absence of large-scale foreign investment, international borrowing, or aid flows, a country must export in order to import. Hence we would expect to find the overall values of any country's exports and imports to be highly correlated over time. This indeed is the case for the four East Asian NICs. Table 7.5 presents the correlations of overall values of the respective manufactured exports and imports between 1965 and 1990. These findings are not unexpected and are in fact typical of any country under most normal circumstances. Only under fairly unusual circumstances would the exports and imports of a country move significantly differently over time. Such circumstances include periods of unusually large foreign aid, perhaps associated with natural disasters, and periods of unusual imbalances in government budgets, causing wide gaps between a country's income and macroeconomic absorption.

Table 7.1 Korean Imports

Product Group	1965 ($000)	1990 ($000)	Average Annual Growth (%)
	From the United States		
Chemicals	39,911	1,734,438	0.16
Resource-based products	4,930	417,022	0.19
Metal manufactures	4,437	269,809	0.17
Nonferrous metals	2,318	182,514	0.19
Textiles	3,286	105,737	0.15
Nonelectrical machinery	8,463	2,297,087	0.25
Electrical machinery	9,019	1,796,914	0.24
Transport equipment	5,387	1,197,918	0.24
Precision instruments	1,435	316,503	0.24
Clothing	2,190	6,008	0.04
Furniture	107	12,243	0.21
Footwear	2	18,167	0.44
Miscellaneous	1,231	290,111	0.24
Total	82,716	8,644,471	0.20
	From the EC		
Chemicals	4,896	1,118,295	0.24
Resource-based products	272	389,489	0.34
Metal manufactures	1,487	345,572	0.24
Nonferrous metals	55	88,833	0.34
Textiles	1,172	254,019	0.24
Nonelectrical machinery	11,755	2,425,738	0.24
Electrical machinery	3,560	642,829	0.23
Transport equipment	10,523	461,359	0.16
Precision instruments	331	189,346	0.29
Clothing	12	83,296	0.42
Furniture	3	23,244	0.43
Footwear	1	11,446	0.45
Miscellaneous	381	219,337	0.29
Total	34,448	6,252,803	0.23
	From Japan		
Chemicals	51,379	2,386,953	0.17
Resource-based products	2,664	665,959	0.25
Metal manufactures	24,840	1,615,392	0.18
Nonferrous metals	3,280	289,259	0.20
Textiles	24,607	557,569	0.13
Nonelectrical machinery	25,578	4,982,917	0.23
Electrical machinery	10,358	3,758,619	0.27
Transport equipment	7,223	483,126	0.18
Precision instruments	3,004	496,874	0.23
Clothing	407	19,136	0.17
Furniture	54	59,401	0.32
Footwear	8	8,444	0.32
Miscellaneous	5,609	778,112	0.22
Total	159,011	16,101,761	0.20

Table 7.2 Taiwan Imports

Product Group	1965 ($000)	1990 ($000)	Average Annual Growth (%)
From the United States			
Chemicals	13,417	1,538,296	0.21
Resource-based products	1,729	294,492	0.23
Metal manufactures	5,498	109,071	0.13
Nonferrous metals	824	361,785	0.28
Textiles	728	64,200	0.20
Nonelectrical machinery	19,173	1,671,999	0.20
Electrical machinery	20,559	2,020,364	0.20
Transport equipment	9,764	1,229,960	0.21
Precision instruments	1,572	173,226	0.21
Clothing	1,372	5,560	0.06
Furniture	19	13,771	0.30
Footwear	1	12,985	0.46
Miscellaneous	1,179	234,390	0.24
Total	75,835	7,730,099	0.20
From the EC			
Chemicals	9,213	830,059	020
Resource-based products	451	234,116	0.28
Metal manufactures	1,129	315,287	0.25
Nonferrous metals	293	75,813	0.25
Textiles	141,082	141,082	0.29
Nonelectrical machinery	11,779	1,237,820	0.20
Electrical machinery	1,216	739,801	0.29
Transport equipment	4,007	973,388	0.25
Precision instruments	294	130,768	0.28
Clothing	2	94,447	0.54
Furniture	7	25,635	0.39
Footwear	1	27,932	0.51
Miscellaneous	790	169,382	0.24
Total	29,410	4,995,530	0.23
From Japan			
Chemicals	32,795	1,789,592	0.17
Resource-based products	4,075	632,150	0.22
Metal manufactures	42,250	1,435,066	0.15
Nonferrous metals	7,805	383,954	0.17
Textiles	11,679	408,961	0.15
Nonelectrical machinery	35,157	3,335,690	0.20
Electrical machinery	25,614	3,807,557	0.22
Transport equipment	28,542	1,290,890	0.16
Precision instruments	2,787	357,025	0.21
Clothing	16	51,483	0.38
Furniture	8	21,081	0.37
Footwear	1	16,203	0.47
Miscellaneous	5,764	843,518	0.22
Total	196,493	14,373,170	0.19

Table 7.3 Singapore Imports

Product Group	1965 ($000)	1990 ($000)	Average Annual Growth (%)
	From the United States		
Chemicals	3,338	677,577	0.25
Resource-based products	2,715	134,009	0.18
Metal manufactures	1,524	129,354	0.20
Nonferrous metals	31	48,614	0.36
Textiles	939	61,511	0.19
Nonelectrical machinery	13,450	2,097,855	0.23
Electrical machinery	2,800	1,857,359	0.31
Transport equipment	3,088	830,497	0.26
Precision instruments	759	171,700	0.25
Clothing	1,121	7,835	0.08
Furniture	12	17,068	0.35
Footwear	2	3,389	0.36
Miscellaneous	4,582	655,867	0.23
Total	34,361	6,692,635	0.25
	From the EC		
Chemicals	15,558	764,454	0.18
Resource-based products	9,754	327,909	0.16
Metal manufactures	9,232	368,024	0.17
Nonferrous metals	2,060	132,175	0.19
Textiles	4,465	114,213	0.14
Nonelectrical machinery	23,101	1,536,550	0.19
Electrical machinery	14,762	1,311,832	0.21
Transport equipment	22,111	666,689	0.15
Precision instruments	1,556	157,848	0.21
Clothing	506	80,756	0.24
Furniture	298	35,620	0.22
Footwear	212	25,057	0.22
Miscellaneous	7,391	429,765	0.18
Total	111,006	5,950,892	0.18
	From Japan		
Chemicals	8,165	530,132	0.19
Resource-based products	10,884	349,498	0.16
Metal manufactures	25,671	803,099	0.15
Nonferrous metals	2,891	207,629	0.19
Textiles	39,433	208,166	0.07
Nonelectrical machinery	9,679	2,222,028	0.25
Electrical machinery	12,076	3,452,016	0.26
Transport equipment	11,116	888,687	0.20
Precision instruments	3,568	269,965	0.20
Clothing	4,028	14,678	0.06
Furniture	129	8,562	0.19
Footwear	84	4,156	0.18
Miscellaneous	7,555	1,242,753	0.24
Total	135,279	10,201,369	0.20

Table 7.4 Hong Kong Imports

Product Group	1965 ($000)	1990 ($000)	Average Annual Growth (%)
From the United States			
Chemicals	25,978	730,179	0.14
Resource-based products	25,856	351,740	0.11
Metal manufactures	2,670	76,080	0.14
Nonferrous metals	1,163	54,727	0.17
Textiles	4,681	139,015	0.14
Nonelectrical machinery	19,042	654,656	0.15
Electrical machinery	17,717	1,043,725	0.18
Transport equipment	1,893	595,840	0.26
Precision instruments	1,618	106,287	0.18
Clothing	5,360	20,868	0.06
Furniture	159	22,144	0.22
Footwear	492	8,112	0.12
Miscellaneous	12,752	330,052	0.14
Total	119,381	4,133,425	0.15
From the EC			
Chemicals	35,235	1,086,623	0.15
Resource-based products	41,776	1,021,527	0.14
Metal manufactures	21,390	324,795	0.11
Nonferrous metals	5,046	98,646	0.13
Textiles	33,893	399,053	0.10
Nonelectrical machinery	41,800	1,025,364	0.14
Electrical machinery	43,642	809,142	0.12
Transport equipment	29,527	348,875	0.10
Precision instruments	5,308	171,366	0.15
Clothing	3,054	403,675	0.22
Furniture	657	82,412	0.21
Footwear	1,428	112,017	0.19
Miscellaneous	16,083	891,620	0.17
Total	278,839	6,775,115	0.14
From Japan			
Chemicals	24,706	839,154	0.15
Resource-based products	25,644	726,350	0.14
Metal manufactures	32,336	615,441	0.13
Nonferrous metals	8,479	171,680	0.13
Textiles	89,926	1,091,810	0.11
Nonelectrical machinery	15,905	1,756,808	0.21
Electrical machinery	28,180	3,180,828	0.21
Transport equipment	9,317	828,464	0.20
Precision instruments	6,262	499,299	0.19
Clothing	4,651	63,860	0.11
Furniture	420	25,173	0.18
Footwear	382	12,526	0.15
Miscellaneous	17,677	2,423,320	0.22
Total	263,885	12,234,713	0.17

Table 7.5 Correlations Between NIC
Exports and Imports

	1968–77	1978–90	1968–90
Taiwan	0.98	0.94	0.97
Korea	0.99	0.98	0.99
Singapore	0.97	0.98	0.98
Hong Kong	0.99	0.97	0.98

However, for a poor country undergoing rapid economic growth and development, as was true for these four NICs for the period under study, another nexus exists which may be reflected in a close association between exports and imports. This is the relationship described in S. Linder's writings and in the economic development literature, especially during the 1960s. The relationship here describes a causality that is in the reverse direction from the overall foreign exchange constraint described in the preceding paragraph. Briefly, in order to maintain or expand its manufactured exports, a NIC may require the import of capital goods, both investment goods and operation imports—spare parts to imported capital goods and nondomestic primary products.[1] Thus, in contrast to the former relationship ("in order to import you must export"), this is exactly the reverse. If the latter relationship exists, with its implied bottlenecks and inflexibilities, then it implies that a statistically significant relationship should be discernible not only between the gross values of import and export flows but also, interestingly, between the exports of certain commodities and the imports of their specific required (direct and indirect) imported inputs.

Whether the historically very rapid economic and export growth experienced by these countries, with their relatively small initial economic base, in fact demanded close relationships between specific exports and their respective required imports is an intriguing question. Such a relationship is typically couched in terms of vulnerabilities. A country facing this situation may be unable to maintain its growth and export expansion if its imports are cut off for some reason (e.g., a sharp shift in its terms of trade). By examining the time structure between exports and imported inputs, the immediacy of the potential vulnerability can be determined. Finally, imports that are especially closely related to a given NIC's successful exports may provide important insight into the nature of the industrialization process that underlies export success. Specifically, it may be possible to identify the relatively critical imports or import categories in the industrialization process of the developing countries. In turn this should help identify the specific import requirements of other next-tier NICs which are on the verge of or intent upon replicating that particular export pattern.

THE RELATIONSHIP BETWEEN IMPORTS AND
MAJOR EXPORT CATEGORIES

In this section we identify the relationships between successful exports for each of the four NICs and their respective imports. The successful exports are defined in two ways. First we rank the exports of each of the four NICs in 1990 and choose the top 10. (The top 10 exports of each of the NICs to the OECD in 1990 are listed in Table 7.6.) Then we note the number of import categories with which each was highly correlated over time. Specifically, we identified the number of individual imports which had a Pearson correlation coefficient greater than 0.90 with each of the 10 top exports. This examination was repeated in turn for lagged imports. As noted previously, the relationship between lagged imports and current exports was examined since it may be that a critical imported capital import may take longer than one or even two years before its effect works through the industrial structure and is translated into any substantial exports.

Table 7.7 presents the average number of imports whose time series had at least a 0.90 coefficient of correlation with each NIC's top exports. To briefly explain Table 7.7, we note from the first entry in the first row that 48.8% of all of Taiwan's imports had a correlation coefficient of at least 0.90 with Taiwan's exports over the period 1968–1977. It is seen from the table that in the earlier period (1968–77) the main exports of the NICs were found to be fairly highly correlated with large numbers of individual import categories.[2] The top 10 exports for Hong Kong, which had the highest import–export association for that period, revealed a very high statistical relationship (a correlation coefficient of at least 0.90) with 53% of all its manufactured imports. Following the Linder model, this would indicate that of the four NICs, Hong Kong's exports of the 1960s and 1970s were most dependent on imported operating capital (i.e., goods in process of raw materials) inputs and as such were most potentially vulnerable to foreign exchange shortages.

During that earlier period, all four NICs' exports were relatively dependent (in the same sense) on imports. Both Taiwan and South Korea's top 10 exports were closely associated with close to 50% of all manufactured import products (48.8% for Taiwan; 47.6% for South Korea). Even Singapore, which was the least dependent at that time, had close statistical relationships between its main exports and over 40% of its manufactured imports.

A clear change occurred by the latter period (1978–87), when the degree of import dependence lessened across the board. For each of the four NICs, the concurrent degree of association of the 10 major export groups with individual import categories declined from its value in the earlier period. The shift away from this import dependence was relatively slight for South Korea (from 47.6% to 41.4%). It was more significant for Taiwan (a decline from 48.8% to 33.8%). It was especially notable for the two city-states, Singapore (from 41.8% to 15.3%) and especially Hong Kong (from 53.1% to 16.4%). Hong Kong, which had the highest "dependency" rank in 1966–77, dropped to third during the 1978–87 period.

Another way to view the phenomenon under investigation is to consider these figures as indirect (inverse) indicators of the domestic value added associated with each of these countries' manufactured exports. In the earlier "take-off" period the

Table 7.6   Top 10 Exports of the NICs to the OECD in 1990

Product Description	SITC	Value ($)
Taiwan		
Office machines	714	5,625,183,000
Clothing	841	3,535,629,000
Toys and games	894	2,789,865,000
Electrical machinery	729	2,607,671,000
Footwear	851	2,235,734,000
Telecommunication apparatus	724	2,181,634,000
Furniture	821	1,529,875,000
Electric power machinery	722	1,329,238,000
Plastic articles	893	1,312,418,000
Nonelectrical machinery	719	1,178,030,000
Korea		
Clothing	841	6,992,039,000
Footwear	851	3,741,653,000
Electrical machinery	729	3,270,140,000
Telecommunication apparatus	724	2,553,788,000
Office machinery	714	2,080,817,000
Musical instruments	891	1,559,454,000
Road motor vehicles	732	1,409,057,000
Toys and games	894	1,026,661,000
Travel goods	831	992,442,000
Nonelectrical machinery	719	744,256,000
Singapore		
Office machines	714	6,433,067,000
Electrical machinery	729	2,248,232,000
Telecommunication apparatus	724	2,219,470,000
Clothing	841	912,078,000
Organic chemicals	512	532,452,000
Musical instruments	891	524,195,000
Electrical power machinery	722	517,374,000
Nonelectrical machinery	719	473,583,000
Crude petroleum-based chemicals	521	221,352,000
Scientific instruments	861	212,342,000
Hong Kong		
Clothing	841	7,793,038,000
Office machines	714	1,536,984,000
Watches and clocks	864	1,088,533,000
Telecommunication apparatus	724	1,080,791,000
Toys and games	894	836,008,000
Jewelry	897	828,544,000
Electrical machinery	729	826,939,000
Scientific instruments	861	540,814,000
Pearls and precious stones	667	536,179,000
Electrical power machinery	722	489,253,000

Table 7.7 Import Dependency Index: Imports Highly
Correlated with Top 10 Exports as a Percentage of All Imports

	Lags, 1968–77			Lags, 1978–87		
	None	One	Two	None	One	Two
Taiwan	48.8	34.3	29.2	33.8	26.0	10.2
South Korea	47.6	40.4	35.4	41.4	25.6	12.2
Singapore	41.0	36.3	32.1	15.8	6.8	4.3
Hong Kong	53.1	40.9	38.0	16.7	8.0	5.2

main exports of these countries to a large extent involved the contribution of relatively small value added to imported manufactures, which were then essentially
reexported. By the 1980s this characterization of their export process became less
realistic or descriptive. Their manufactured exports were less likely to be essentially
reworked reexports. Again, this was especially true for Hong Kong and (to a lesser
degree) Singapore. It was less true for South Korea, which demonstrated the highest
ranking of the import dependency index, with indices over 40% in both periods.
Taiwan falls somewhere in the middle of this process. Its import dependency index
dropped from 48.8% to 33.8%—a far more significant a drop than South Korea's.

INTRA-INDUSTRY TRADE: A FIRST LOOK

This finding sheds light on a different issue fully discussed in Chapter 9—the
phenomenon of intra-industry trade. One of several generally argued hypotheses
explaining the proliferation and expansion of intra-industry trade is the tendency for
multinational corporations to increasingly engage in internationally specialized vertical integration. The findings here suggest that over the past two decades, such a
tendency on the part of multinational corporations did not significantly dominate
overall NIC trade patterns, especially during the relatively recent 1980s. On the
contrary, the figures in Table 7.6 point to a tendency to greater national industrial
integration, incorporating increasingly greater portions of the production process in
the single-country exporters rather than resorting to greater international intra-industry specialization.[3]

Focusing on the columns within each time period, relating to various import lags,
it is noted that in every case, the greatest number of (very) high correlations between
exports and imports occur with nonlagged, contemporaneous imports. In each case,
fewer high correlations were found when imports were lagged one year, and fewer
still when these were lagged two years. This indicates that in general, in Linderian
terms, the inputs are more in the nature of operating imports than of fixed-capital
investment goods. Hence a generally short "roundaboutness" is indicated. When
the individual products underlying the averages in Table 7.6 are examined, very few
exceptions to this rule were found.[4]

IMPORTS AND THE MOST RAPIDLY GROWING EXPORTS

It is possible that the export–import relationships may be dominated by traditional exports. Although not dynamically growing, such exports may still constitute a large portion of all exports through historic inertia or other factors, such as the Multifiber Agreement. If this is the case, the conclusions drawn previously may describe the current or past situation while having little relevance to future developments. In order to examine and possibly correct for this, we repeated the analysis focusing not on the top 10 exports in dollar value but rather on the top 10 fastest growing exports; that is, the 10 export categories (which consisted of at least $1 million at the start of the period examined) exhibiting the largest percentage growth rates during the respective period. Table 7.8 presents the results.

Comparing the first (contemporaneous import) columns in Table 7.8 with those in Table 7.7, one may draw the following conclusions. First, with the one exception of Hong Kong, the import dependency indices associated with the growth industries (i.e., the most rapidly growing export categories) were lower than those associated with the currently successful top 10 exports. The implication of this tendency is that over time, the relationship between NIC exports and specific imported items will tend to lessen. Judging from the later period examined (1978–87), which is most relevant to projections into the near future, this tendency is seen to be especially applicable for Singapore, whose marginal index of 7.8% in Table 7.8 is roughly only half of its average index of 15.8% in Table 7.7. It is found to be applicable also for South Korea, whose marginal index of 30.7% is roughly three-fourths its average index of 41.4%. On the other hand, the findings for Taiwan and Hong Kong suggest that the current indices of export–import association will remain relatively constant over the near future. In both cases the marginal indices are practically identical to those of the average indicators.

A quick examination of the comparisons of the marginal with the average indices in the earlier period (1968–1977) supports our inferences. We find that in every case where the index in Table 7.8 is lower than that in Table 7.7, the average in the following period (1978–87) in Table 7.7 fell. This is especially notable for Singapore. Here the 1968–77 marginal indicator of 14.5% was much lower than the average 41.0%—and indeed a very substantial drop was found, from 41.0% to 15.8%.

Finally, which particular imports were especially highly correlated with the most

Table 7.8 Import Dependency Index: Imports Highly Correlated with 10 Most Rapidly Growing Exports as a Percentage of All Imports

	Lags, 1968–77			Lags, 1978–87		
	None	One	Two	None	One	Two
Taiwan	41.8	28.4	25.2	32.8	21.6	9.9
South Korea	45.8	38.8	33.1	30.7	20.8	8.5
Singapore	14.5	5.7	5.8	7.8	6.2	5.0
Hong Kong	66.3	58.2	51.0	17.2	7.0	4.9

rapidly growing exports? An answer to this question would be of interest in promoting our understanding of the structural underpinnings of the growth process which underlay the dramatic export drives of the NICs. It is also of interest since it may provide valuable strategic marketing data concerning the likely import growth areas in the near-NICs, to the extent that they are "following in the footsteps" of the NICs in their own relatively rapid rise to NIC status.

In each time period (1968–77 and 1978–87), each import could be found to be highly correlated at a maximum with all 10 of the most rapidly growing exports and at a minimum, with none. Appendix Tables 7.1 and 7.2 indicate the actual number of such observed cases of high correlations for each of the 101 imported manufactured products for each NIC in each of the two time periods.

CRITICAL IMPORTS

Table 7.9 lists the all-NIC imports which proved to be highly correlated with the largest number of the most rapidly growing exports of all the NICs combined, for the two subperiods. The table identifies those imported products that were es-

Table 7.9 Import Categories Most Closely Correlated
with the Top 10 Growth Exports, All NICs

1968–77		1978–87	
SITC	Product	SITC	Product
641	Paper	655	Special fabrics
729	Electrical equipment NES	551	Perfumes
891	Musical instruments	892	Printed matter
714	Office machines	532	Dying extracts
514	Other inorganic chemicals	891	Musical instruments
675	Iron and steel hoops	714	Office machines
861	Scientific instruments	664	Glass
533	Pigments	831	Travel goods
554	Soaps	861	Scientific instruments
654	Lace	729	Electrical equipment NES
642	Paper articles	641	Paper
894	Toys	722	Electrical power machinery
513	Inorganic chemicals	657	Tapestries
899	Manufactured articles	642	Paper articles
674	Sheets	581	Plastic materials
698	Metal manufactures NES	531	Synthetic dyes
581	Plastic materials	893	Plastic articles NES
663	Mineral manufactures NES	554	Soaps
722	Electrical power machinery	862	Photo supplies
684	Aluminum	663	Mineral manufactures NES
694	Nails	512	Organic chemicals
862	Photo supplies	533	Pigments
541	Pharmaceuticals	895	Office supplies NES
512	Organic chemicals	621	Rubber materials

Note: NES = not elsewhere supplied.

pecially critical to the earlier export drive and those that underpinned the export drive of the later period. By comparing the two lists, we will gain interesting insight concerning the differences between the two periods' export drives. We also can identify those import groups that are likely to become important in the domestic markets of the ASEAN near-NICs. Since, as demonstrated in Chapter 8, the respective NIC export vectors cannot be said to be significantly homogeneous from a statistical point of view, our analysis will proceed separately for each of the individual NICs. Tables 7.10 through 7.13 list those imports most closely correlated with the 10 fastest growing exports of each NIC. The data underlying these tables are presented in Appendix Tables 7.1 and 7.2.

Taiwan's Import Market

We now ask the following question: Which of the products highly correlated with the fastest growing exports in the 1978–87 period were also highly correlated with the fastest growing exports of the earlier period? And to the extent that they were not, what type of structural shift is indicated?

First, a fairly stable situation is depicted. Of the highest ranked 17 import categories (those highly correlated with either 10 or 9 of the most rapidly growing exports during 1978–87), 12 may be seen to have also been highly correlated with a relatively large number of the fastest growing exports during the earlier period. These import categories are:

714	Office machines and computers
892	Printed matter
541	Pharmaceuticals
532	Dying extracts
551	Perfumes
642	Paper articles
861	Scientific and measuring instruments
641	Paper and paperboard
531	Synthetic dyes
533	Pigments
663	Mineral manufactures NES
729	Electrical equipment NES

These import categories were all correlated with at least 9 of the 10 fastest growing export categories in 1978–87. In turn, each was highly correlated with at least 8 such rapidly growing export categories in the earlier period. The significance of the high proportion of imports in the latter period which were also included in the corresponding list of the earlier period is that, despite the somewhat rapid changes which took place in Taiwan's export vector between these two periods (see Table 2.5), Taiwan's import market remained rather stable for many of the export-related imports. This suggests that the import products listed above will probably retain or increase their proportion of all imports in the coming decade.

Table 7.10 Manufactured Import Categories (Three-Digit SITC Rev 1) Most Closely Correlated with the Most Rapidly Growing Exports of Taiwan

1966–77		1978–87	
SITC	Product	SITC	Product
895	Office supplies NES	655	Special fabrics
674	Sheets	714	Office machines
861	Scientific instruments	892	Printed matter
641	Paper	651	Textile yarn
531	Synthetic dyes	541	Pharmaceuticals
514	Other inorganic chemicals	532	Dying extracts
714	Office machines	862	Photo supplies
729	Electrical equipment NES	551	Perfumes
541	Pharmaceuticals	642	Paper articles
532	Dying extracts	861	Scientific instruments
892	Printed matter	664	Glass
554	Soaps	641	Paper
726	Medical electrical equipment	531	Synthetic dyes
513	Inorganic chemicals	533	Pigments
621	Rubber materials	663	Mineral manufactures NES
654	Lace	729	Electrical equipment NES
533	Pigments	851	Footware

The smaller group of four import categories found at the top of the rankings in 1978–87 but not in so ranked in the earlier period are

655 Special fabrics
651 Textile yarn
664 Glass
851 Footwear

The changes in relative rank that occurred here are dramatic. The first, special fabrics, is among the highest four categories in the later period (correlated with 10 of the 10 most rapidly growing exports). During the earlier period, it was highly correlated with only one of the then most rapidly growing exports, its rank thus being higher than 60 of 101. Textile yarn's case is even more dramatic. Again, in the later period it is among the top four categories; in the earlier period it had not been highly correlated with even one of the most rapidly increasing exports—thus occupying a rank higher than 68. Glass and footwear similarly rose from the bottom of the rankings to the very top.

It is clear that textile-related products dominate this group. If we were to include items correlated with eight export categories, then SITC 656 (textile articles NES), which was correlated with none in the earlier period, would join the list. Clearly, Taiwan's rapidly growing exports of the later period began to rely on imported textile-related inputs, a situation which was not true during the earlier period. This finding would suggest that indeed within the textile industry, Taiwan was experiencing a shift to greater intra-industry specialization during the 1980s. Since textiles still comprise a large proportion of Taiwan's total manufactured exports and are likely to do so for the foreseeable future (if only due to market share rigidities associated with the Multifiber Agreement), Taiwan is likely to provide a promising market for various textile subcategories during the coming decade.

Korea's Import Market

The picture describing the Korean situation differs considerably from that of Taiwan. In the case of South Korea, very little stability is found in the interperiod rankings. Of the 19 products that were highly correlated in 1978–87 with at least 8 of the top 10 growth exports, only 5 were to be found in the higher respective rankings during 1966–1977. These "stable" products were

891 Musical instruments
514 Other inorganic chemicals
893 Plastic articles NES
897 Jewelry
674 Universals, plates, and sheets

All of the other 14 products had been highly correlated with relatively few of the then most rapidly growing exports, falling thirty-fifth or higher in the rankings of that earlier period. There are several noticeable characteristics about this group of imports. First, none fall within the SITC 7 category (machinery and transport

Table 7.11 Manufactured Import Categories (Three-Digit SITC Rev 1) Most Closely Correlated with the Most Rapidly Growing Exports of South Korea

1966–77		1978–87	
SITC	Product	SITC	Product
891	Musical instruments	667	Pearls
729	Electrical equipment NES	891	Musical instruments
513	Inorganic chemicals	655	Special fabrics
675	Hoops	665	Glassware
641	Paper	621	Rubber materials
674	Sheets	633	Cork manufactures
514	Other inorganic chemicals	514	Other inorganic chemicals
652	Cotton fabrics	893	Plastic articles NES
724	Telecommunications equipment	895	Office supplies NES
894	Toys	842	Fur clothing
531	Synthetic dyes	653	Other fabrics
685	Lead	629	Rubber manufactures NES
521	Mineral tar	551	Perfumes
864	Clocks	657	Tapestries
683	Nickel	532	Dying extracts
698	Metal manufactures NES	666	Pottery
654	Lace	897	Jewelry
714	Office machines	674	Sheets
682	Copper	831	Travel goods

equipment). They all tend to be low-tech products. Nine of these products fall within the SITC 6 category, (resource-based products). Of these, three are textile categories, and a fourth (841) is clothing.

When one considers that of the 12 highest ranked imports of the earlier period (1966–78), 4 import categories could be considered to be relatively sophisticated, perhaps high tech—729, electric equipment NES; 724, telecommunication equipment; and 513 and 514, inorganic chemicals—the contrast with the later period becomes clear. Whereas South Korea's exports of the earlier take-off period were in part associated with and dependent on relatively sophisticated capital goods imports, during the more recent period they became increasingly associated with low-value-added, resource-based imported inputs. Like Taiwan, the observed pattern is consistent with a trend to greater intra-industry specialization, with an emphasis on the higher-value-added, sophisticated end of the respective industries' production lines.

The relatively unstable pattern in the interperiod rankings suggests that an understanding and correct estimation of the magnitude of the progressive shift to lower line products in its export-related import mix is critical for those who would forecast or project South Korea's imports into the next decade.

Singapore's Import Market

As noted earlier, the degree of association between top-growth Singapore exports and imports increased significantly from the earlier take-off period to the later period encompassing primarily the 1980s. It might also be useful to note that as compared to the other NICs, Singapore's top growth exports were found to be relatively independent of "critical" or any specific imports. In the earlier period, the largest number of top growth exports with which any of the imports were found

Table 7.12 Manufactured Import Categories (Three-Digit SITC Rev 1) Most Closely Correlated with the Most Rapidly Growing Exports of Singapore

1966–77		1978–87	
SITC	Product	SITC	Product
663	Mineral manufactures NES	664	Glass
533	Pigments	642	Paper articles
642	Paper articles	726	Medical electrical equipment
725	Domestic electrical equipment	714	Office machines
684	Aluminum	652	Cotton fabrics
531	Synthetic dyes	723	Electrical distributing equipment
891	Musical instruments	893	Plastic articles NES
667	Pearls	729	Electrical equipment NES
581	Plastic materials	892	Printed matter
861	Scientific instruments	682	Copper
641	Paper	821	Furniture
664	Glass	512	Organic chemicals
897	Jewelry	655	Special fabrics
732	Road motor vehicles	722	Electrical power machinery

Table 7.13 Manufactured Import Categories (Three-Digit SITC Rev 1)
Most Closely Correlated with the Most Rapidly Growing Exports of Hong Kong

1966–77		1978–87	
SITC	Product	SITC	Product
812	Plumbing articles	892	Printed matter
899	Manufactured articles NES	641	Paper
821	Furniture	663	Mineral manufactures NES
697	Household equipment	726	Medical electrical equipment
678	Pipes	581	Plastic materials
698	Metal manufactures NES	532	Dying extracts
631	Plywood boards	655	Special fabrics
719	Machines NES	893	Plastic articles NES
642	Paper articles	722	Electrical power machinery
895	Office supplies NES	831	Travel goods
611	Leather	551	Perfumes
714	Office machines	862	Photo supplies
		891	Musical instruments
		657	Tapestries
		541	Pharmaceuticals
		861	Scientific instruments
		513	Inorganic chemicals

to be highly correlated was 3 (of 10). In the later period, the corresponding number
was 6 (and even this relatively low number was found for only 2 (of 101) imported
manufactures.

Like South Korea, and unlike Taiwan, very little stability was found in the
interperiod rankings. Of the top 14 ranked imports for 1978–87, only 2 were also in
the top 14 during the earlier period (664, glass, and 642, articles made of paper or of
paper pulp). Unlike Taiwan, many of the imports newly associated with top growth
exports in the 1980s were sophisticated, high-tech, nonelectrical and electrical
machinery categories. In retrospect, this is not unexpected, since a relatively small
economy such as Singapore's cannot hope to be in a position to provide the comprehensive selection of industrial infrastructure necessary for its rapid and broad-based
industrial and export drive.

Hong Kong's Import Market

Like South Korea and Singapore, Hong Kong's export-related imports underwent a
significant change between the two periods examined here. Not a single import
category of the top-ranked 10 imports from the 1966–77 period are to be found
among the top-ranked 19 import categories of the later period. As is true with
Singapore, the newly "export-significant" Hong Kong manufactured imports represent a broad spectrum of sophistication and capital intensiveness. Unlike Singapore,
as indicated earlier, the trend in Hong Kong was generally toward a less import-
dependent export structure. Indeed, the number of rapidly growing exports for
which high correlations were found for each import category roughly halved on
average between the two periods.

FREQUENCY COUNT OF IMPORT CATEGORIES WITH HIGH CORRELATIONS WITH RAPIDLY GROWING EXPORT CATEGORIES

Appendix Tables 7.1 and 7.2 indicate the number of times each of the 101 import categories had a correlation coefficient of 0.9 or higher with one of the 10 most rapidly growing export categories. Note that the range of these numbers is from 10 (when the import category was very highly correlated with each and every one of the top 10 growth exports) to 0 (when it was highly correlated with none).

Appendix Table 7.1   Number of Top Growth Exports with Which Each Imported Product was Highly Correlated, 1966–1977

SITC	Product	Taiwan	Korea	Singapore	Hong Kong
512	Organic chemicals	7	8	1	9
513	Inorganic chemicals	8	9	1	9
514	Other inorganic chemicals	9	9	2	9
515	Radioactive elements	0	0	0	6
521	Mineral tar	8	8	0	0
531	Synthetic dyes	9	9	3	4
532	Dying extracts	8	7	1	9
533	Pigments	8	8	3	9
541	Pharmaceuticals	9	6	1	9
551	Perfumes	8	6	0	0
553	Cosmetics	0	0	0	0
554	Soaps	8	8	2	9
561	Fertilizers	0	0	0	0
571	Explosives	0	7	0	8
581	Plastic materials	6	8	3	9
599	Chemicals NES	8	2	0	3
611	Leather	6	8	0	10
612	Leather manufactures	7	5	2	9
613	Fur skins	2	7	1	9
621	Rubber materials	8	0	1	9
629	Rubber manufactures NES	7	2	2	9
631	Plywood boards	3	0	0	10
632	Wood manufactures NES	2	0	2	0
633	Cork manufactures	0	3	0	0
641	Paper	9	9	3	9
642	Paper articles	8	6	3	10
651	Textile yarn	0	0	0	0
652	Cotton fabrics	3	9	1	9
653	Other fabrics	8	3	0	9
654	Lace	8	8	2	9
655	Spcial fabrics	1	4	1	4
656	Textile articles NES	0	0	1	7
657	Tapestries	7	0	2	9
661	Cement	4	0	2	9
662	Construction materials	1	0	2	9
663	Mineral manufactures NES	8	6	3	9
664	Glass	1	6	3	9

Appendix Table 7.1 Continued

SITC	Product	Taiwan	Korea	Singapore	Hong Kong
665	Glassware	7	6	2	9
666	Pottery	0	1	1	9
667	Pearls	0	3	3	9
671	Pig iron	1	0	0	0
672	Ingots	4	6	0	1
673	Bars and rods	0	7	0	8
674	Sheets	9	9	0	9
675	Hoops	8	9	2	9
676	Rails	0	0	0	0
677	Wire	8	8	0	8
678	Pipes	0	7	0	10
679	Castings NES	0	0	0	0
681	Silver	0	5	0	0
682	Copper	7	8	1	8
683	Nickel	0	8	0	0
684	Aluminum	7	8	3	8
685	Lead	0	9	0	0
686	Zinc	3	0	0	0
687	Tin	0	8	0	0
689	Nonferrous metals NES	0	4	2	0
691	Metal structures	0	0	0	0
692	Metal containers	0	0	0	9
693	Wire products	1	3	0	8
694	Nails	8	8	1	9
695	Tools	8	6	1	9
696	Cutlery	7	0	1	2
697	Household equipment	1	0	1	10
698	Metal manufactures NES	8	8	1	10
711	Power machinery	5	6	1	7
712	Agricultural machinery	0	0	0	0
714	Office machines	9	8	2	10
715	Metalworking machinery	0	7	2	9
717	Textile machinery	0	1	0	3
718	Special machines	8	1	0	9
719	Machines NES	2	7	2	10
722	Electrical power machinery	7	8	2	9
723	Electrical distributing equipment	6	8	0	9
724	Telecommunication equipment	1	9	2	9
725	Domestic electrical equipment	8	0	3	9
726	Medical electrical equipment	8	1	2	9
729	Electrical equipment NES	9	9	2	9
731	Railway vehicles	0	0	1	1
732	Road motor vehicles	5	1	3	9
733	Other road vehicles	0	0	0	1
734	Aircraft	2	0	2	0
735	Ships	0	0	0	1
812	Plumbing articles	7	1	1	10
821	Furniture	4	0	0	10
831	Travel goods	0	7	2	9

(*continued*)

Appendix Table 7.1 Continued

SITC	Product	Taiwan	Korea	Singapore	Hong Kong
841	Clothing	0	0	1	9
842	Fur clothing	0	1	0	9
851	Footware	0	1	2	7
861	Scientific instruments	9	7	3	9
862	Photo supplies	7	8	2	9
863	Developed film	0	2	2	6
864	Clocks	6	8	1	9
891	Musical instruments	8	9	3	9
892	Printed matter	8	6	1	9
893	Plastic articles NES	2	8	1	9
894	Toys	8	9	1	9
895	Office supplies NES	9	2	2	10
896	Works of art	0	3	0	9
897	Jewelry	0	8	3	7
899	Manufactured articles NES	8	8	1	10

Appendix Table 7.2 Number of Top Growth Exports with Which Each Imported Product was Highly Correlated, 1979–1987

SITC	Product	Taiwan	Korea	Singapore	Hong Kong
512	Organic chemicals	7	7	3	0
513	Inorganic chemicals	0	3	2	5
514	Other inorganic chemicals	0	9	0	1
515	Radioactive elements	0	6	0	0
521	Mineral tar	0	0	0	0
531	Synthetic dyes	9	6	0	4
532	Dying extracts	9	8	0	5
533	Pigments	9	4	0	4
541	Pharmaceuticals	9	1	0	5
551	Perfumes	9	8	3	5
553	Cosmetics	0	0	0	0
554	Soaps	7	7	0	4
561	Fertilizers	0	4	0	0
571	Explosives	0	0	0	0
581	Plastic materials	6	7	1	5
599	Chemicals NES	3	0	0	0
611	Leather	0	0	0	0
612	Leather manufactures	0	6	0	1
613	Fur skins	0	0	0	0
621	Rubber materials	3	9	0	4
629	Rubber manufactures NES	0	8	0	1
631	Plywood boards	7	0	0	0
632	Wood manufactures NES	0	1	0	0
633	Cork manufactures	0	9	0	0
641	Paper	9	5	1	5
642	Paper articles	9	0	6	4
651	Textile yarn	10	5	0	0
652	Cotton fabrics	0	4	5	1
653	Other fabrics	0	8	0	4
654	Lace	4	5	0	0

Appendix Table 7.2 Continued

SITC	Product	Taiwan	Korea	Singapore	Hong Kong
655	Special fabrics	10	9	3	5
656	Textile articles NES	8	2	0	0
657	Tapestries	6	8	0	5
661	Cement	0	0	0	0
662	Construction materials	0	0	0	1
663	Mineral manufactures NES	9	3	1	5
664	Glass	9	4	6	2
665	Glassware	0	9	0	1
666	Pottery	1	8	0	4
667	Pearls	0	9	0	0
671	Pig iron	0	0	0	0
672	Ingots	0	0	0	0
673	Bars and rods	2	0	0	0
674	Sheets	0	8	0	4
675	Hoops	1	0	0	1
676	Rails	0	0	0	0
677	Wire	2	5	1	4
678	Pipes	0	0	0	0
679	Castings NES	0	0	0	0
681	Silver	0	0	0	0
682	Copper	0	1	3	1
683	Nickel	0	0	0	0
684	Aluminum	0	0	2	0
685	Lead	0	0	3	0
686	Zinc	0	0	0	0
687	Tin	0	0	0	0
689	Nonferrous metals NES	4	0	1	0
691	Metal structures	0	0	0	0
692	Metal containers	0	0	0	0
693	Wire products	0	0	0	0
694	Nails	1	0	1	3
695	Tools	6	1	0	4
696	Cutlery	0	1	0	4
697	Household equipment	5	0	0	3
698	Metal manufactures NES	0	2	0	0
711	Power machinery	0	0	1	0
712	Agricultural machinery	0	0	0	0
714	Office machines	10	4	5	2
715	Metalworking machinery	0	0	0	4
717	Textile machinery	4	3	0	4
718	Special machines	0	0	0	0
719	Machines NES	2	6	0	4
722	Electrical power machinery	7	5	3	5
723	Electrical distributing equipment	0	0	5	0
724	Telecommunication equipment	5	0	1	0
725	Domestic electrical equipment	8	0	0	1
726	Medical electrical equipment	5	0	5	5
729	Electrical equipment NES	9	4	4	4
731	Railway vehicles	0	0	0	0

(*continued*)

Appendix Table 7.2   Continued

SITC	Product	Taiwan	Korea	Singapore	Hong Kong
732	Road motor vehicles	5	6	0	0
733	Other road vehicles	8	0	0	0
734	Aircraft	0	0	0	1
735	Ships	0	0	0	0
812	Plumbing articles	1	0	0	2
821	Furniture	0	5	3	0
831	Travel goods	8	8	0	5
841	clothing	7	4	0	4
842	Fur clothing	0	8	0	0
851	Footware	9	3	0	0
861	Scientific instruments	9	6	1	5
862	Photo supplies	9	4	0	5
863	Developed film	0	3	0	0
864	Clocks	6	0	0	1
891	Musical instruments	8	9	0	5
892	Printed matter	10	3	4	6
893	Plastic articles NES	0	9	4	5
894	Toys	0	3	0	0
895	Office supplies NES	7	9	0	0
896	Works of art	0	0	1	1
897	Jewelry	0	8	0	0
899	Manufactured articles NES	0	0	0	0

NOTES

1. The terminology is from Linder (1961, 1967).

2. The top 10 exports of each of the NICs in 1990 comprised the following percentages of their total manufactured exports of that year: Taiwan 63.3%, South Korea 69.5%, Singapore 86.8%, and Hong Kong 78.4%.

3. This tendency is supported by the generally declining trends noted for the "product specialization" indices during the latter period for most of the NICs (chapter 9).

4. For example, for Taiwan, of the top 10 exports, a single one was found which had a higher import dependence index for once-lagged, as compared to contemporaneous, imports (SITC 831, travel goods, handbags, etc.), while only one other had a slightly higher index for twice-lagged as compared with once-lagged imports (SITC 631, plywood boards).

REFERENCES

Linder, S. 1961. *An Essay on Trade and Transformation*. New York: Wiley.
————. 1967. *Trade and Trade Policy for Development*. New York: Praeger.

8

The Comparative Homogeneity
of the East Asian NIC Exports
# of Similar Manufactures

The emergence of the newly industrializing countries as highly dynamic exporters represents a dramatic departure from the widely accepted poor prognosis for the development process generally associated with overpopulated, undercapitalized, vicious-circle dynamics during the 1950s and 1960s. Though the conventional wisdom attributes NICs' success to export-promoting, free-market strategies, recent work sheds doubt on many of these generally accepted propositions (e.g., Bradford).

In much of the literature, the East Asian NICs (the "Gang of Four" or the "four tigers") have been treated as though they were a single, homogeneous economic entity. All four grew rapidly, penetrating manufactured export markets in the United States and the OECD so dramatically as to displace Japan from many labor-intensive sectors; in turn they became targets of explicit protectionist sentiment in the importing countries. All four followed an export-driven growth strategy. Of course, the Chinese heritage—either ethnic or cultural—plays an important role in each of these countries as well.

Yet we know that these four countries differ greatly from one another in ways which, a priori, ought to affect their export compositions and responses. Singapore alone of the four has consciously altered its industrial composition by raising real wages. The degree of structural change and average growth rates have differed significantly between these countries.[1]

Indeed, in an earlier paper Kellman tested the hypothesis that the export responses of the four tigers to changes in the U.S. market, after taking into account domestic supply capabilities, were identical. That test was performed for various groups of manufactures for the decade 1968–77. The findings were rather surprising. Though in general the null hypothesis (homogeneity) was rejected, it could not be rejected for one important subset of manufactures—the relatively sophisticated groups of R&D-intensive products and machinery. No statistical difference could be found in the manner in which the exports of these product groups responded to U.S. market demand cycles in Singapore, Hong Kong, South Korea, or Taiwan. For these products, but not for the more traditional labor-intensive products, it appeared as though the four tigers' export drive to the United States was highly coordinated.

This chapter updates and expands upon the earlier paper. We utilize data extending over a longer period of time and employ a theoretically more acceptable model. In addition, we explore various hypotheses that may explain the hitherto unobserved trade phenomenon.

THE EMPIRICAL TEST

The model chosen is a standard import demand model. It hypothesizes that changes in the imports of products into the United States from a given exporting country may be explained primarily in terms of changes in the U.S. gross national product (GNP) and changes in the real exchange rate of the exporting country. The actual specification estimated was

$$\log(X_i) = a + b_1\log(GNP_u) + b_2\log(RXR)$$

where X_i is the value of manufactured exports from country i to the United States, GPN_u is the gross national product of the United States, and RXR is the real exchange rate, calculated as the exchange rate expressed as U.S. dollar equivalents times the ratio of the two countries' consumer price indices.

The actual estimation utilized a two-year polynomial distributed lag structure on the real exchange rate, since it has been established in the literature that the relative price effect on world trade tends to lag by roughly two years in most cases, often yielding a perverse J effect, in which a currency devaluation or depreciation initially leads to a worsened trade balance; and only subsequently results in an improved balance of payments.

$$\log(X_i) = a + b_1 \log(GNP_u) + b_2 \log[RXR(0)] \div b_3 \log[RXR(-1)] + b_4 \log[RXR(-2)]$$

The results for all manufactures for each of the exporting countries, as summarized in Table 8.1, are reasonable. The Keynesian effect of U.S. income growth on imports is positive and significant throughout.

Because of the generally poor Durbin–Watson statistics, the actual calculations

Table 8.1   Estimated Coefficients from Unrestricted Ordinary Least Squares (OLS)

	b_1	b_2	b_3	b_4	R^2
Hong Kong	1.72	−0.07	0.13	−0.96	0.99
	(52.40)	(1.00)	(0.60)	(1.50)	
South Korea	2.55	0.04	1.03	0.11	0.96
	(19.50)	(0.10)	(1.20)	(0.10)	
Singapore	3.09	−0.83	2.94	−1.93	0.95
	(12.90)	(0.20)	(2.40)	(0.90)	
Taiwan	2.50	−0.42	0.46	−1.93	0.98
	(10.70)	(0.80)	(0.60)	(2.50)	

Note: Figures in parentheses are t statistics.

Table 8.2 Estimated Parameters from Pooled
OLS Regressions

b_1	b_2	b_3	b_4	R^2
3.05	−0.16	−0.04	−0.001	0.98
(35.70)	(0.60)	(1.50)	(0.06)	

Note: Figures in parentheses are *t* statistics.

upon which the reported results rely were estimated with a generalized least square
(GLS) second-order autocorrelation correction, which tended to improve the esti-
mates in terms of the indications of serial correlation.[2]

The results for the first pooled sample are summarized in Table 8.2. The findings
indicate that every 10% increase in the U.S. GNP resulted in a 30% increase of
imported manufactures from the four East Asian NICs. The price responsiveness of
the NICs' exports was not statistically significant. This accords with general findings in the literature. We examine this price responsiveness for individual product
groupings in the following section.

To determine whether these pooled reactions are in fact representative or typical
of each and every one of the four exporters, we examine the relationships between
the unrestricted country OLS regressions against the pooled regression results. The
F test compares the sum of squared residuals (SSR) from the pooled model (SSR*p*)
with the sum of squared residuals from the individual country regressions (SSR*u*):

$$F = \frac{(\text{SSR}_p - \text{SSR}_u)/df_1}{\text{SSR}_u/df_2}$$

where df_1 is the restricted degree of freedom. If the computed *F* test does not exceed
the tabulated value for the respective degrees of freedom, then the null hypothesis
(homogeneity) cannot be rejected.[3]

The tabulated critical values are $F(15, 65) = 1.85$ at the 5% level and 2.37 at the
1% level. The actual calculated *F* value for all manufactured exports was 2.41.
Hence the null hypothesis was rejected. The four tigers did not react in tandem or
unison to changing demand and relative prices in the international market. The
results of the *F* tests are summarized in Table 8.3.

THE TEST FOR SPECIFIC PRODUCT CATEGORIES

The same test was then performed for each of the following product groups:[4]

Traditional (i.e., the main traditional labor-intensive products: textiles, clothing,
simple consumer goods)

Textiles

Clothing

Consumer goods

Machinery

Transport equipment

R&D intensive (A)

R&D intensive (B)

30% or more U.S.-owned subsidiaries

3% or less U.S.-owned subsidiaries[5]

The results are striking. Despite the expanded time period and the changed specification (including an explicit account of the relative price effects), the major finding of the earlier paper is replicated. All manufactured NIC exports to the United States are characterized by heterogeneity. That is, changes in U.S. demand (as represented here by U.S. GNP) and in real exchange rate (Table 8.4) elicit unique responses in the export volumes of each of the four tigers. The F statistic of 2.41 leads us to reject the hypothesis of uniformity.

This particular finding is sensible, and not especially unexpected, given the very real differences in economic structures and policies of the four. However, the next finding is indeed exciting. On a regular basis it was found that heterogeneity, or country-specific export response, was characteristic of traditional exports but not true for more sophisticated manufactures.

The F statistics for machinery, transport equipment, and R&D-intensive products (A and B) are all smaller than the critical values. The inference to be drawn here is that the four tigers did indeed act in unison for these products.

DISCUSSION

As far as we know, with the exception of Kellman, this is the first time the homogeneous export responses of the four East Asian NICs' exports to the United States

Table 8.3 *F* Statistics for Selected Product Groups

Product Group	F Statistic
All manufactures	2.41
Traditional	14.20
Textile	15.02
Clothing	11.72
Consumer goods	19.84
Machinery	0.36
Transport equipment	1.69
R&D intensive (A)	0.64
R&D intensive (B)	0.31
U.S. subsidiaries greater than 30%	1.11
U.S. subsidiaries less than 3%	15.89

Table 8.4 Real Exchange Rate Effects
for Selected Product Groups

Product Group	b_2	b_3	b_4
Traditional	−0.20	−0.07	−0.01
	(6.80)	(2.40)	(0.50)
Textiles	−0.20	−0.04	−0.04
	(4.50)	(0.80)	(0.90)
Clothing	−0.17	−0.08	−0.02
	(5.60)	(2.70)	(0.50)
Consumer goods	−0.64	0.05	0.25
	(13.40)	(1.10)	(5.20)
Machinery	−0.57	0.12	0.16
	(7.10)	(1.50)	(1.90)
Transport equipment	−0.26	−0.02	0.10
	(2.70)	(0.20)	(1.00)
R&D intensive (A)	−0.37	0.07	0.12
	(6.10)	(1.20)	(1.90)
R&D intensive (B)	−0.53	0.13	0.09
	(6.00)	(1.40)	(1.00)

Note: Numbers in parentheses are *t* statistics.

have been demonstrated in the literature. The explanation for this observed homogeneity is not clear. Several possibilities are explored here. In general, two polar explanations may be offered for the phenomenon—a "collusive" and a "competitive" approach. Presumably, any explanation of the observed intercountry uniformity will fit one of these two approaches. We offer four tentative hypotheses.

The first, a collusive hypothesis, suggests that the firms producing the less traditional, more highly R&D-intensive products in the four producing countries are in a position to collude. One possible explanation for this may be that a high proportion of these particular products tend to be produced in wholly owned subsidiaries of U.S. corporations. Since the same large corporations would control similar producing units in each of the four exporting countries, they could easily coordinate the export responses. Without exploring this possibility at length, we did explore the proposition that a higher degree of inter-NIC uniformity is to be found in the products of largely owned subsidiaries of U.S. multinationals. This was done by selecting two groups of products. One group contained manufactured goods which are largely produced in U.S.-owned subsidiaries. If at least 30% of U.S. imports of a product were produced in U.S.-owned subsidiaries, the good would be included in the first category. The second group contained manufactures less influenced by U.S. control. If less than 3% of U.S. imports of a particular good were produced in U.S.-owned subsidiaries, that product would fall into the second category. The appendix lists the product groups in each category. We then performed the same *F* test described earlier for each of these two groups. To support our hypothesis, we would expect to find a low *F* statistic for the over 30% group and a high one for the under 3% group. The findings are the last two rows of Table 8.3. In fact, the null hypothesis (of exporter homogeneity) is strongly supported for the groups of products made largely by U.S.-owned subsidiaries (*F* = 1.11) and is strongly rejected for the group in which foreign-owned subsidiaries play an especially small role (F = 15.89).

The second, a competitive solution, suggests that the explanation of the observed trends lies in the nature of the technology utilized in each industry. Those products produced by new technologies, as proxied by high inputs of research and development in their cost structures, may all tend to be utilizing the state of the art (in terms of both physical and human capital). Since their cost structures would not be influenced greatly by heavy physical capital or unskilled labor components, their marginal cost structures would tend to be very similar; this would explain the observed intercountry homogeneity. To examine this proposition, we applied the F test to two conceptual product groupings: high-tech and low-tech. The high-technology industries are those defined as R&D intensive. Two separate product groupings were used, drawn from two different sources. The low-tech end of the industrial spectrum may be considered to be the traditional product groups. The results, again summarized in Table 8.3, support this working hypothesis as well, since both R&D-intensive products groups had small F values, whereas the low-tech products groupings had relatively high F values.

A third possible explanation, again in the collusive mode, would focus on the effects of quantitative restrictions on the part of the United States. Presumably policies such as the Multifiber Agreement, which divides the U.S. import market among the textile exporters, would strongly affect the uniformity of export response. We tested this proposition by dividing the traditional products into two subgroups, those subject to the MFA (textiles and clothing) and those not (consumer goods). If the MFA played a critical role in explaining the observed phenomenon, then we would expect to find a clear distinction in the findings related to these two groups of products. In fact, however, the findings in Table 8.3 demonstrate that being subject to the MFA per se had no discriminatory effect on the homogeneity of export responses. Textiles and clothing as well as consumer goods had F statistics well above the critical value.

A final, competitive, possibility is that newer, less traditional exports are more sensitive to price signals than are traditional exports. This may be due to various factors, such as factor rigidities in the nonmodern sector, often described in development models. A finding in support of this proposition would be that the exports of traditional goods do not respond (logically and significantly) to changes in real exchange rates, whereas nontraditional products groups do. The relevant statistics appear in Table 8.4, which summarizes only the price effects, leaving out the income (GNP) coefficients.

The findings are mixed but suggestive. In all product groups, a perverse effect was encountered with the concurrent exchange rate. With the single exception of clothing, the negative effect remained intact for the one- and two-year lags for the traditional products. However, for each and every nontraditional category, the initial negative reaction proved to be merely the beginning of the classic J curve. By the first or second year's lag, the export response became "rational" (i.e., a real depreciation called forth a systematic increase in exports). This finding supports the proposition that the newer, less traditional export sectors in the four tigers tend to be more price responsive. As such, they would tend to respond to changes in world prices with a greater degree of uniformity than would be observed for those traditional products, where price sensitivity is generally lacking. If this interpretation is correct, then one would expect in the future to find a growing homogeneity in the export pattern of these countries, since the proportion of less traditional products has been growing rapidly throughout the period studied, as is clear in Table 8.5. Exports from the four East Asian NICs—the four tigers—tend to respond to U.S. demand in the classic, Keynesian manner and tend to be generally insensitive to changes in relative prices (real exchange rates). An examination of the export reactions of each country with the pooled sample revealed a basic lack of homogeneity in the responses. This, in and of itself, is only of mild interest, since, as evident in Table 8.5, the export compositions of these countries differ considerably from one another.

However, when subsamples of similar product groupings were examined, a surprising finding emerged. For products other than the traditional groups (textiles, clothing, and simple consumer goods) the homogeneity hypothesis could not be

Table 8.5 Percentage Distribution of NIC Exports to the United States, Selected Product Groups

Product Group	Hong Kong	South Korea	Taiwan	Singapore
1966				
Traditional	67.9	56.5	44.6	73.6
Textiles	9.0	11.4	9.7	20.1
Clothing	31.6	26.8	23.2	53.5
Consumer goods	27.4	18.4	11.7	0.1
Machinery	8.8	1.9	14.9	0.1
Transport equipment	0.7	0.2	0.2	0.1
R&D intensive (A)	17.5	3.9	20.3	0.2
R&D intensive (B)	9.8	2.0	15.8	0.0
1976				
Traditional	66.8	59.9	56.3	15.6
Textiles	5.4	2.0	2.2	1.3
Clothing	38.6	40.4	34.6	10.1
Consumer goods	22.9	17.4	19.6	4.1
Machinery	13.1	7.6	22.0	22.4
Transport equipment	0.3	0.3	1.5	0.6
R&D intensive (A)	23.2	20.3	30.5	74.7
R&D intensive (B)	17.5	9.4	23.8	30.5
1986				
Traditional	62.2	52.7	49.1	13.9
Textiles	2.1	3.0	2.3	0.1
Clothing	40.5	32.5	24.5	9.1
Consumer goods	20.7	17.2	22.4	4.7
Machinery	19.8	18.7	24.4	4.7
Transport equipment	0.5	7.3	3.7	2.4
R&D intensive (A)	29.5	29.6	29.2	78.1
R&D intensive (B)	23.8	19.2	22.3	58.2

Note: Product groups are not mutually exclusive.

rejected. The four exporters were reacting to changes in U.S. income and to exchange rate changes in a unified and apparently coordinated manner.

Four hypotheses—two competitive and two collusive—were explored as possible explanations of this phenomenon. The first examined the relationship between multinational subsidiary status and intercountry homogeneity of export response. A strong relationship was observed to exist here. The second focused on the role of modern, state of the art, R&D-intensive technology. Again, the R&D embodiment proved to be an important discriminant with respect to intercountry homogeneity of export response. The third hypothesis examined the role of comprehensive quantitative restrictions, in particular the Multifiber Agreement. This was done by seeking differences in export responses between traditional product groups subject to the MFA and groups not so subject. In this case, no clear effect of the MFA was found. Finally, a fourth hypothesis was explored. This examined the relationship between price sensitivity and intercountry homogeneity. The finding here was weak but suggestive. The products groups in which intercountry homogeneity was discovered were also found to respond to international price signals, though with a delay, in a theoretically logical manner. This was not true for the other product groups.

Appendix Table 8.1   Product Group
Classifications (SITC Rev 1)

SITC	Product Group
Textiles[a]	
651	Textile yarn and thread
652	Cotton fabric, woven
653	Textile fabric, other than cotton
654	Tulle, lace, embroidery
655	Special textile, fabrics
656	Made-up articles
657	Floor covering
Clothing[a]	
841	Clothing (except fur)
842	Fur clothing
851	Footwear
Consumer Goods[a]	
553	Perfumery and cosmetics
554	Soaps
696	Cutlery
821	Furniture
831	Travel bags
891	Musical instruments
892	Printed matter
893	Articles of plastic
894	Toys
895	Office supplies
897	Jewelry
899	Manufactured NES

Appendix Table 8.1 Continued

SITC	Product Group
	R&D Intensive (A)
513	Inorganic chemicals
514	Other inorganic chemicals
541	Pharmaceuticals
581	Plastic materials
571	Explosives
862	Photographic supplies
	R&D Intensive (B)
51	Chemicals
541	Pharmaceutical goods
561	Manufactured fertilizers
581	Plastic materials
711	Power-generating machinery
714	Office machines
719	Macninery NES
722	Electrical power machines
724	Telecommunications equipment
729	Electrical measuring and controlling equipment
734	Aircraft
86	Photographic and optical equipment
891	Records, tapes
	Machinery
711	Power-generating machinery
712	Agricultural machinery
714	Office machines
715	Metalworking machinery
717	Textile machinery
719	Machinery NES
722	Electrical power machinery
723	Electrical distributing equipment
724	Telecommunications equipment
725	Domestic electrical equipment
	Transport Equipment
731	Railroad vehicles
732	Road motor vehicles
733	Road vehicles NES
734	Aircraft
735	Ships
	Over 30% U.S. MNC-Owned
513	Inorganic chemicals
571	Explosives
629	Articles of rubber NES
714	Office machines
725	Domestic electrical equipment

ªTraditional products. (*continued*)

Appendix Table 8.1   Continued

SITC	Product Group
731	Railroad vehicles
732	Road motor vehicles
734	Aircraft
862	Photographic supplies
Under 3% U.S. MNC-Owned	
611	Leather
632	Wood manufactures NES
652	Cotton fabric, woven
654	Tulle, lace, embroidery
655	Special textile fabrics
661	Lime and cement
664	Glass
665	Glassware
677	Iron and steel castings
682	Copper
684	Alumina
685	Lead
686	Zinc
687	Tin
693	Wire products
831	Travel goods
841	Clothing (except fur)
842	Fur clothing
851	Footwear
897	Jewelry
899	Manufactures NES

NOTES

This chapter was derived from M. Kellman and P. C. Y. Chow, "The Comparative Homogeneity of the East Asian NIC Exports of Similar Manufactures," *World Development* 17, no. 2 (1989):267–73. *World Development* is published by Pergamon Press Ltd., Oxford, United Kingdom.

 1. See Bradford (1987), Table 1.

 2. See Kmenta (1971), section 12.2.

 3. See Maddala (1977), chapter 14, for a detailed description of the test.

 4. The actual product composition of each of the groups is detailed in Appendix 8.1. The study utilized two different commodity group definitions for R&D intensiveness. The first group (A), replicating the classification of the earlier paper, utilized the definition from Kellman and Carney (1981). The second group (B) utilized a definition from the U.S. Department of Commerce (1983, appendix A).

 5. The variable is the proportion of all imports into the United States produced in U.S.-owned subsidiaries. Its source is Lavergne (1983).

REFERENCES

Bradford, C. 1987. "Trade and Structural Change: NICs and Next Tier NICs as Transitional Economics." *World Development* 15, no. 3:229–316.

Kellman, M. 1987. "The Compositional Cohesion of the Four Tigers' Export Drive to the United States." *Journal of International Economic Integration* 2, no. 2:125–39.

Kellman, M., and R. Carney. 1981. *Patterns and Determinants of Manufactured Export Success of the New Industrialized Countries 1965–1979*. Final Report to the Bureau of International Labor. Washington, D.C.: Department of Labor.

Kmenta, H. 1971. *Elements of Econometrics*. New York: Macmillan.

Lavergne, R. 1983. *The Political Economy of U.S. Tariffs—An Empirical Study*. New York: Academic Press.

Maddala, G. S. 1977. *Econometrics*. New York: McGraw-Hill.

U.S. Department of Commerce. 1983. *An Assessment of U.S. Competitiveness in High Technology Industries*. Washington, D.C.: U.S. Department of Commerce.

9

Intra-Industry Trade:
Diversification Versus Specialization

The researcher attempting to understand the source of NIC export success must consider the role of product specialization. This insight—that successful economic development is rooted in the extent and degrees of product specialization—can be traced to Adam Smith. It is generally inferred from the Ricardian model of comparative advantage that success in exports is associated with a certain degree of specialization in production of those products in which the exporting countries enjoy comparative productivity advantages vis-à-vis their potential trading partners. Subject to constraints of diminishing returns, one would expect that as market forces are increasingly allowed to play their role in the determination of export compositions, one would find over time a growing degree of such specialization. The Ricardian model suggests that the direction of causality runs from specialization to export success. The greater the ability of a country to direct its resources to those products or sectors in which it enjoys comparative advantage (subject to overall world market absorptive capacity), the greater will be its exports at any point in time.

It is generally believed that protection and other trade-distorting policies tend to move a country away from its competitive optimal production mix. It follows that given a cross section, one would expect to find, ceteris paribus, that those countries whose trade policies are more "liberalized," in the sense of allowing market forces to determine their export compositions, would tend to demonstrate a greater degree of specialization in their export vectors.

An alternative hypothesis, however, associates relative degrees of specialization not with relative market forces but rather with relative levels of development. A very poor country may demonstrate a very high degree of specialization (or a very low degree of diversification) simply because its industrial infrastructure cannot support the production and export of a broad range of products; as its economy grows and develops, it will diversify—that is, its observed level of product specialization in exports will tend to decrease. As noted by Balassa, "The degree of specialization and diversification of manufactured exports . . . may be explained by reference to the size of domestic markets."[1]

The tendency for exports from poor but rapidly growing countries to become more diversified over time, as their "representative demands" tend over time to approximate those of their major industrialized trading partners, is supported as well by the Linder hypothesis (outlined in Chapter 7). Indeed it is possible that both these factors play their respective roles in determining the extent and changes in the degree of specialization in export compositions of a nation. The four NICs shared an unusually similar and uniform experience in the manner in which their respective patterns of export specialization and diversification changed over the period studied. It is argued here that these patterns may provide an important clue to why this particular group of poor countries succeeded whereas so many others (including those like the Philippines with very high levels of education and human capital endowments) failed. The NICs grew rapidly during the period studied in this book, *and* they tended either to operate within the context of relatively free market forces or to move fairly consistently in that direction during the period studied. Thus they can furnish excellent data for a case study of the relative explanatory power of each of these two hypotheses.

These two hypotheses are briefly stated as follows:

The "Balassa effect": Observed patterns of export specialization merely reflect and follow an increasingly sophisticated productive base or, alternatively,

The "Ricardo effect": Observed patterns may be concomitants and explainers of export success.

One way to test these two is to examine the relationship between inter-industry, and intra-industry export specialization patterns. If the only causal relationship between economic development and export specialization is the Balassa effect, then with economic development, one would tend to expect to find a growing degree of diversification both across and within industries. However, if the Ricardo effect is operating, one would expect to observe divergent patterns. As the NICs grow, their increasingly sophisticated economic base will allow for both a broader range of exports and an increased ability to focus on relatively narrower levels of comparative advantages within respective industries. This in turn would lead to an expectation of growing intra-industry specialization.

We use the coefficient of variation of respective countries' export vectors as the measure of specialization. The higher the measure, the more specialized is the export vector. This may be intuitively explained by noting that if a country exports 100 products but 90% of them came from 1 product category and the remaining 10% was scattered among the remaining 99 products, a very high degree of variability would obtain. On the other hand, if its exports were greatly diversified, so that 1% of its exports was from each of the 100 product categories, an examination would find a very low coefficient of variation.

Two separate tests were made. The first utilized all of the 101 products (at the three-digit SITC level of aggregation). Coefficients of variation and changes in this statistic over time would tend to represent both inter-, and intra-industry shifts.[2] The second test utilized data aggregated at the 13-industry level, as represented in the tables throughout the book. Though we expect to find lower levels of specialization at this more aggregated level of observation, we may clearly interpret changes in this measure as focusing on purely inter-industry changes. Thus a comparison of the results from these two examinations will allow us to note the separate effects of inter- and intra-industry shifts in relative specialization over the period examined.

INTRA-INDUSTRY CHANGES IN EXPORT SPECIALIZATION: THE DISAGGREGATED PRODUCT SAMPLE

Table 9.1 indicates several cross sections of the respective coefficients of variation of the exports for each NIC. Figure 9.1 illustrates two of these cross sections, one for 1966 and the other for 1990. It is clear that the degree of product specialization generally tended to decrease over time, as the coefficient of variation for 1990 is lower than that for 1966 for all NICs except Singapore. This was especially true for Taiwan and Korea. In 1966 the degree of product specialization was especially high for Hong Kong and low for Taiwan. In 1990 Hong Kong and Singapore had specialization indicators clearly higher than those of Taiwan and Korea.

Figures 9.2 through 9.5 indicate the annual respective measures of export product specialization for each of the NICs. They refer to the full 101-product sample, thus embodying both inter- and intra-industry changes.

Figure 9.2 indicates the changes in South Korea's measure of export specialization. The figure clearly shows that from the mid-1960s until the first OPEC shock of the early 1970s Korea's export composition exhibited an increasingly specialized pattern, but from the early 1970s a persistent and clear tendency to product diversification characterized its export compositions—a tendency that continued to the early 1990s.

Figure 9.3 depicts the changes in the index of export specialization of Taiwan over the same period. Over time, the pattern of changing product specialization for Taiwan's exports closely resembles that of Korea. In general, the mid- to late 1960s saw a growing tendency to specialization; since then the opposite tendency has predominated.

Figure 9.4 shows Singapore's pattern of product specialization over the same time period. Singapore's pattern was at least qualitatively similar to those of Taiwan and South Korea in the earlier period. During the mid- and late 1960s, there was a notable increase in the degree of product specialization in Singapore's exports, much like that observed for Korea and Taiwan. Likewise, the early 1970s saw the same sharp increase in product diversification. However, from the mid-1970s the pattern for Singapore diverges sharply from that observed for the first two countries.

Table 9.1 Coefficients of Variation, 101 Products

	Korea	Taiwan	Singapore	Hong Kong
1966	388.4	335.3	385.2	423.6
1970	406.7	340.8	454.6	405.7
1975	345.5	319.9	348.9	497.3
1980	301.7	254.3	372.6	408.1
1985	283.2	228.7	345.5	409.6
1990	262.6	216.6	437.5	411.8

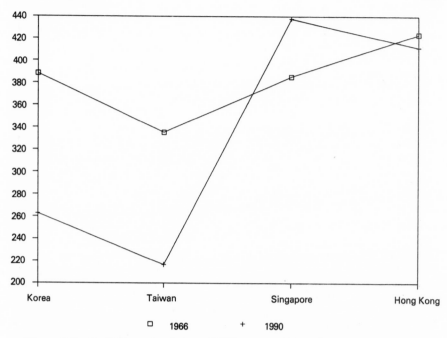

Figure 9.1 Coefficient of variation of NIC exports, 101 products, 1966 and 1990.

In Singapore there is a clear resumption of the movement toward specialization and away from diversification in the product composition of its exports. This tendency was especially clear from 1985 to 1990.

Figure 9.5 presents Hong Kong's pattern of product diversification. Hong Kong proves to be clearly different from each of the other NICs. To some extent its experience may be seen as a mirror image of Singapore's. In the mid- to late 1960s, there was a slight tendency to greater diversification. This trend was sharply reversed in the early 1970s, when its measure of specialization soared. From the mid-1970s, however, this last tendency was reversed, and (like Taiwan and Korea) its exports became clearly more diversified. The 1980s showed no clear trend, as the degree of product specialization (or diversification) fluctuated with some slight indication of an increased tendency to specialization after 1987.

INTER-INDUSTRY CHANGES IN EXPORT SPECIALIZATION: THE AGGREGATE INDUSTRY SAMPLE

Table 9.2 presents the measures of specialization for the aggregated 13-industry sample. They may therefore be interpreted as represented solely industry-by-industry, or inter-industry, levels and changes.

Comparing the inter-industry indices in Table 9.2 with the more disaggregated inter- and intra-industry indices of Table 9.1, we note that the latter are larger. As

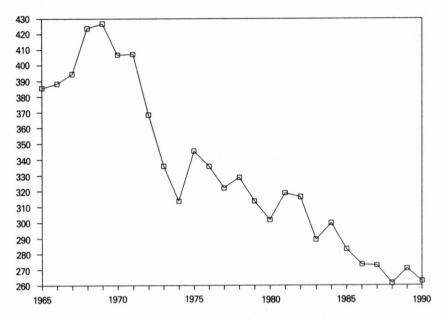

Figure 9.2 Coefficient of variation of Korea's exports, 1965–90.

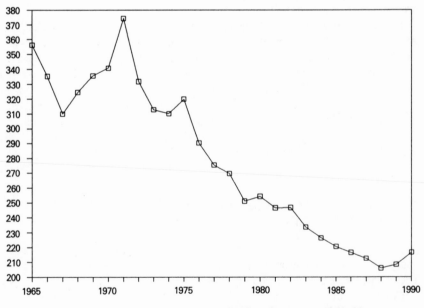

Figure 9.3 Coefficient of variation of Taiwan's exports, 1965–90.

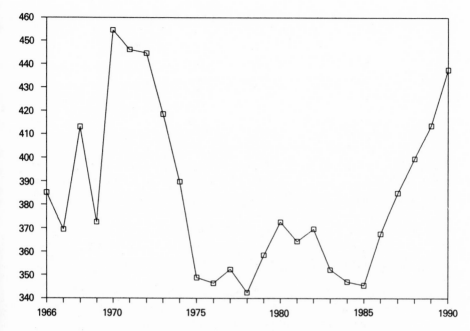

Figure 9.4 Coefficient of variation of Singapore's exports, 1966–90.

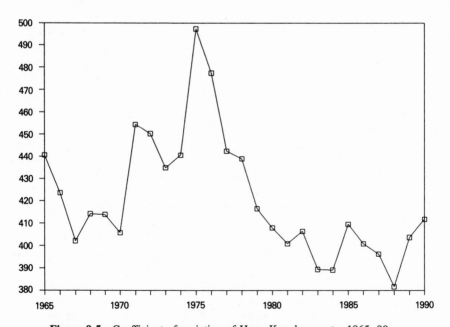

Figure 9.5 Coefficient of variation of Hong Kong's exports, 1965–90.

Table 9.2 Coefficients of Variation, 13 Products

	Korea	Taiwan	Singapore	Hong Kong
1966	134.6	120.4	134.4	163.0
1970	130.5	117.4	178.1	161.2
1975	136.0	109.2	166.1	179.7
1980	106.7	92.7	196.2	164.2
1985	102.3	82.0	167.0	160.7
1990	89.3	86.9	177.6	156.6

expected, the aggregation process decreased the degree of variability between observations. Since Table 9.1 does include the effects of variability within the 13-product groups whereas Table 9.2 does not, we may interpret the relationship between the figures in the two tables as a rough indication of the effect of intra-industry (i.e. within the 13-product groups) variations in product diversification or specialization. Table 9.3 indicates the ratio of the coefficients of variation from the inter- and intra-industry sample (from Table 9.1) to those from the inter-industry sample (Table 9.2).

With the exception of Singapore, the relative weight of intra-industry product variation remained fairly constant throughout the 25-year period studied. Thus the effects of intra-industry specialization did not affect the rankings obtained from observing purely inter-industry coefficients of variation. From this one may infer that the main specialization–diversification effects found in these countries' exports were inter-industry effects, with the within-industry changes in specialization affecting the product mixes only marginally.

Comparing the ratios in Table 9.3 across countries, one may conclude that during the period 1970–85 the relative importance of compositional shifts within product groups (i.e, intra-industry shifts) was relatively greater in Taiwan and Korea than in Singapore and Hong Kong. Another way of putting it is that during that period, specialization was along clear industry lines for Hong Kong and Singapore. During the critical mid- to late 1960s, this ratio increased in both South Korea (from 2.89 to 3.12) and Taiwan (from 2.78 to 2.90), while for the two city-states the relative importance of inter-industry specialization increased as the ratios fell (from 2.87 to 2.55 for Singapore; from 2.60 to 2.52 for Hong Kong).

In the 15-year period from 1965 to 1980 the relative weight of intra-industry specialization remained fairly constant in all of the NICs except Singapore. In Singapore the relative importance of intra-industry specialization compared to inter-industry specialization fell continuously during this period. From a value of 2.87 in 1966, the ratio of Singapore's two measures (from Tables 9.1 and 9.2) fell to 1.90 in 1980. This shows a clear tendency to a sharper demarcation by industry in its pattern of specialization during this period. In the other three NICs no such clear pattern emerged, and the relative weights of inter- and intra-industry specializations were essentially trendless. By the 1980s the relative weight of inter-industry specialization in Singapore was the highest of all NICs. Whereas in terms of the disaggregated product groups (Table 9.1) Hong Kong registered the highest overall measure of export product specialization, Singapore ranked highest when only industry differences were taken into account (Table 9.2).

Since the ratios (Table 9.3) tended to remain constant for all except Singapore, it follows that the pattern of specialization one would observe utilizing only the inter-industry sample (13 aggregated product groups) would be similar to those observed using the full 101-product sample for all countries except Singapore. Figures 9.6 and 9.7 illustrate this point for Taiwan and Singapore.

Figure 9.6 clearly indicates that in the case of Taiwan the two patterns are practically identical. The explicit consideration of the full 101-product sample did not yield any new or different patterns not observable from the 13-product sample. However, in the case of Singapore the two patterns differ considerably. Between 1970 and 1985, the degree of product specialization did not change appreciably for Singapore when only inter-industry changes were allowed for (Figure 9.7*a*). However, when the intra-industry shifts were allowed to register their effects (Figure 9.7*b*) a sharp shift toward product diversification is indicated for the same period. Thus during the period 1970 through the mid-1980s, when little systematic change characterized inter-industry export patterns, Singapore did experience a significant shift to intra-industry diversification in its export product mix.

To summarize, during the period 1965–90, during which these four NICs experienced unprecedented growth and export expansion, all except Hong Kong experienced a measure of increased specialization. This was true whether focusing on the more or the less detailed product sample. The second regularity which is observed in these graphs is that all NICs experienced cyclical, or alternating, patterns of greater specialization followed or preceded by shifts toward greater product diversification. As noted previously, both South Korea and Taiwan experienced a growing export product shift into a narrower range of both inter- and intra-industry export specialization during the take-off period of the mid- to late 1960s followed by a relatively sharp move in the opposite direction. The same pattern was observed for Singapore (a tendency toward specialization in the mid- to late 1960s followed by a relatively sharp period of especially intra-industry diversification in the 1970s). After the mid-1970s, their respective experiences diverged, as the first two countries continued on their trend to greater diversification through the 1980s, whereas Singapore shifted gears once more and moved toward increased (inter-industry) specialization once more from the mid- to late 1970s. However, as noted, in this case a renewed tendency toward greater product specialization took effect from the mid-1970s. The 1980s saw a universal shift in all NICs toward a greater degree of inter-industry diversification.

THE BALASSA VERSUS THE RICARDO EXPLANATION OF SPECIALIZATION TRENDS

These observations suggest several hypotheses. First, it would appear that neither the Balassa nor the Ricardo effect explains in full the export growth–product specialization nexus that typified the NIC experience. Second, it is feasible that one explanation for the unusual degree of success the NICs had in attaining and maintaining their economic growth throughout this period of world recession and oil price dislocations was precisely the cyclical, or alternating, pattern we observed.

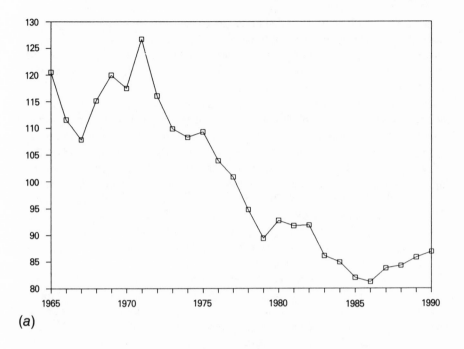

(a)

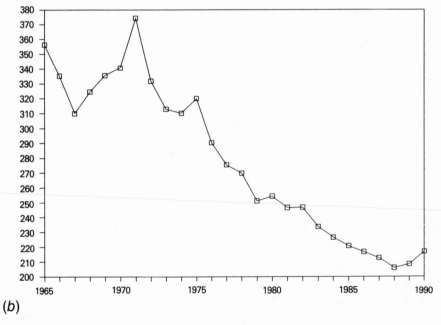

(b)

Figure 9.6 Coefficient of variation of Taiwan's exports, 1966–90. (a) Aggregated (13-product) sample; (b) disaggregated (101-product) sample.

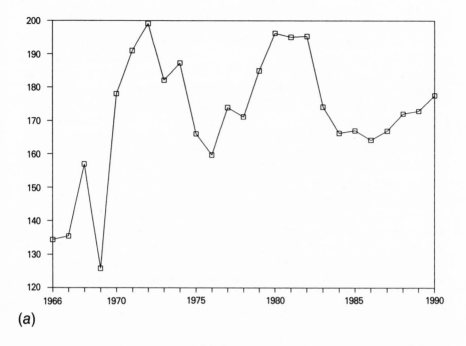

(a)

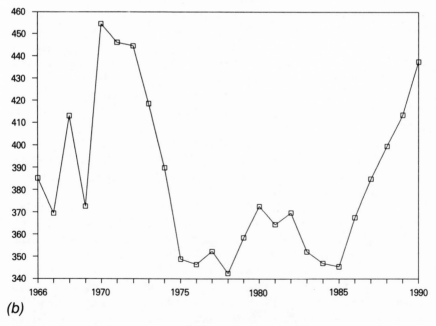

(b)

Figure 9.7 Coefficient of variation of Singapore's exports, 1966–90. (a) Aggregated (13-product) sample; (b) disaggregated (101-product) sample.

Each exporter experienced an identifiable period during which comparative advantage was actively being exploited, as respective exports focused on increasingly narrower product definitions. This is a period consistent with a Ricardian exploitation of potential comparative advantage. It is notable that South Korea, Taiwan, and Singapore *began* their export-driven growth with an initial move to greater specialization. This obviously neither proves nor guarantees that a conscious move to increase a country's export specialization in the "correct" product mix will ensure long-term economic growth dividends. However, it is interesting that this is precisely what characterized the export drive of these three NICs during the very rapid expansion, or take-off, period of the 1960s.

The contrary experience of Hong Kong may be considered the exception which proves the rule. Alone of all four NICs, by the mid-1960s Hong Kong was already a world-class exporter in a relatively narrow range of products. It is likely that the early association of "export take-off" with a notable increase in export product specialization had occurred in Hong Kong (as it had in the others) but that this happened earlier than the mid-1960s. However, not only were Hong Kong and Singapore smaller, but they were more "advanced" in their export structure at that early period. From the findings of chapter 4 we may judge that Hong Kong was already ahead of the other NICs in the sense that its export pattern more closely resembled that of Japan.

We may draw an interesting inference from Hong Kong's and Singapore's patterns. In both a period of diversification is preceded and followed by a period of increased specialization. Singapore, like Hong Kong, may be considered to be at a more advanced stage in the export–development nexus than were South Korea and Taiwan. We note this from Table 4.2, in which Singapore demonstrated an export pattern in the mid-1960s significantly more similar to Japan's. A working hypothesis suggested here is that after a certain level of specialization and export intensity had been achieved, the specialization–diversification pattern may perhaps not be a one-time straight-line lead–lag phenomenon (as it appears to be in the cases of Taiwan and South Korea). Indeed, the cyclical pattern of movement first in one direction, then in the other, may hold a key to the success demonstrated by these countries.

As noted earlier, by comparing and contrasting the patterns found to describe the 13 aggregate industries, with those describing the behavior of the relatively disaggregated (inter- and intra-industry) sample of 101 product categories, one may be able to separate the two effects.

Let us begin with South Korea. The crucial take-off period of the mid- to late 1960s did see a divergence between the inter- and intra-industry patterns. The 13-industry sample demonstrated a clear tendency toward greater diversification, whereas the 101-industry sample, which includes intra-industry shifts, clearly indicated increased specialization. The situation observed here was one in which the move to greater specialization did indeed occur within industry groups at the same time that a broader range of industries came "on line" as effective exporters. The same combination of Ricardo and Balassa effects is noted in the case of Taiwan during that same critical take-off period. On the other hand, for both city-states, Hong Kong and Singapore, the inter- and intra-industry patterns coincided during this period and subsequently as well. This suggests that the inter-industry shifts toward and away from specialization (or diversification) either were complemented by like shifts or at least were not countered by opposite shifts within industry groups. This may merely reflect the relatively small size of the city-state economies (relative to the other two NICs), or it may indicate that once these countries reach a relatively high level of export product specialization, further shifts in these patterns reflect inter-industry changes (since not much potential for intra-industry specialization remains).

INTRA-INDUSTRY TRADE: IMPLICATIONS FOR FUTURE TRADE TRENDS

It is conventionally argued that whereas intra-industry trade is an increasingly important portion of trade among the industrialized countries, this is not likely to be the case for trade between developed and developing countries. The intuitive explanation is that trade in differentiated products is expedited by similar incomes, tastes, and relative factor proportions, as is generally true among the developed, or industrialized, countries. On the other hand, the large income and relative factor price differences which typify the developed–developing country spectrum lead to a deemphasis of such trade, and rather support a more classical inter-industry specialization pattern. However, studies have indicated that intra-industry trade is present in developing country trade, and specifically in NICs–developed country trade.[3]

Three somewhat competing hypotheses explain the existence and (as we shall note later) growing relative importance of intra-industry elements in the trade between NICs and developed countries. The first, consistent with the Linder hypothesis, argues that the underlying explanation lies in the relatively converging income and hence taste levels. Over the period examined in this book—from the mid-1960s to the late 1980s—growth rates in the Asian NICs consistently exceeded those of the OECD countries; there was a concomitant convergence of income levels of the NICs with those of the richer trade partners, hence the range of "representative goods" they tended to export and import would be expected to widen and encompass an increasingly broader commodity grouping and an increasingly larger proportion of all bilateral trade between these two groups of countries. The second explanation is more conventional, deriving from the presence (and growing importance) of trade in manufactured products incorporating product differentiation, scale economies, and technological factors, that is, the same general factors which have been found to explain the growing weight of intra-industry trade among developed countries. As the NICs' markets grow, and as their productive capacity grows in scale and sophistication, they develop tastes for differentiated products along with an industrial capability to produce them. Finally, the third explanation simply points to growing international vertical integration of multinational corporations, which increasingly tend to ship components to subsidiaries in the NICs for assembly and then ship back the final assembled product to the home markets.

NIC–INTRA-INDUSTRY TRADE: THE RECENT RECORD

Table 9.4 summarizes the intra-industry trade (IIT) indices for each of the NICs in each of the major OECD markets for selected years. These indices are the percentage share of each NIC–OECD market trade flow attributable to intra-industry trade. We utilize the measure developed by Grubel and Lloyd:

$$\text{IIT}_y = \left[\frac{1 - \text{abs}(X_y - M_y)}{X_y + M_y} \right] \times 100$$

where X_y is the export of product y from an NIC to an OECD trading partner and M_y is the import of the same NIC of product y from the same OECD trading partner. The full set of IIT indices for the 12 trade vectors (4 NICs with 3 major OECD markets) for each of the annual observations from 1965 to 1990 are presented in Appendix Table A9.1.

When we examine the mid-1960s—the take-off period—it is clear that Hong Kong was most involved in intra-industry trade. In this sense Hong Kong may be considered the most "advanced" of the NICs at that critical period. With the exception of Singapore, the United States was the market most extensively associated with IIT, whereas Japan's market accommodated very little such trade. At that time, the ranges involved were the following. While 22.4% of all Hong Kong's trade with the United States involved intra-industry trade, only 0.4% of Singapore's trade with Japan consisted of such two-way trade. The one exception to the general pattern noted was Singapore's trade with the EC. While exhibiting the smallest IIT proportion in its trade with both the United States and Japan, it had the highest IIT proportion in its EC trade.

A likely explanation, which will be submitted to a formal test in the following section, is that the pattern observed in the mid-1960s reflects the pattern of operation of multinational enterprises. The relatively high share of U.S. trade probably reflects the dominance of U.S.-based multinational corporations (MNCs) in that period. The Singaporan–EC "anomaly" undoubtedly reflects the remaining British economic influence in its former colony. The very low IIT ratios associated with NIC–Japan trade flows in that period reflect the relative absence of Japan-based MNCs back in the 1960s as well as the well-known and documented tendency for Japan to export high-value-added, relatively sophisticated finished manufactures

Table 9.3   Relative Importance of Intra-Industry
Variations in Product Specialization

	Korea	Taiwan	Singapore	Hong Kong
1966	2.9	2.8	2.9	2.6
1970	3.1	2.9	2.6	2.5
1975	2.5	2.9	2.1	2.8
1980	2.8	2.7	1.9	2.5
1985	2.8	2.8	2.1	2.5
1990	2.9	2.5	2.5	2.6

Table 9.4 NIC Intra-Industry Trade, 1966–90 (%)

	South Korea	Taiwan	Singapore	Hong Kong
With the United States[a]				
1966	8.6	18.8	7.1	22.4
1970	14.1	24.2	30.2	19.5
1980	19.3	22.8	26.4	26.2
1990	33.1	30.1	47.5	29.7
With the EC				
1966	4.6	7.4	14.6	20.6
1970	6.7	13.8	13.7	21.4
1980	23.1	22.8	38.0	26.9
1990	27.9	30.1	41.4	37.9
With Japan				
1966	3.9	1.9	0.4	7.5
1970	17.1	11.7	1.0	12.5
1980	36.1	21.5	8.1	10.6
1990	38.1	37.2	21.7	12.4

[a] These results correspond closely with the unweighted IIT indices reported in Manrique (1987, table 2, p. 486).

and import (especially from LDCs and NICs) semiprocessed, labor-intensive components and semiprocessed goods.

The quarter century from the mid-1960s to 1990 saw a clear shift toward intra-industry trade across the board. By 1990 IIT constituted over 40% of Singapore's trade with both the United States and the EC while Taiwan's and South Korea's two-way trade constituted from a fifth to a quarter of all their manufacture trade with both these markets.

Perhaps the most dramatic shift occurred with respect to the Japanese market. Whereas in 1966 practically no two-way trade existed between either Taiwan or South Korea and Japan, by 1987 roughly 30% of both NICs' trade with Japan was classified as IIT. In fact, by late 1990 the intra-industry trade of both Taiwan and South Korea with Japan was higher than their two-way trade with either the United States or the EC. We have here a clear indicator of the meshing and interlocking of these East Asian markets. By the early 1990s the conventional view of the NICs as mere providers of industrial components for Japan's economic machine is clearly outdated.

FACTORS UNDERLYING NIC–INTRA-INDUSTRY TRADE

Can the observed patterns be explained in terms of conventional hypotheses? It has been noted that intra-industry trade has been a growing portion of world trade in recent decades.[4] Furthermore, as indicated earlier, several studies have found this to characterize both LDC–LDC and NIC–DC trade flows.

The article by Manrique cited earlier clearly illustrates that such trade was relatively important and grew proportionately from the mid-1960s to the early 1980s between the four (East Asian) NICs and the United States. The discussion that follows expands upon the results presented in that study by updating the calculations to 1990, by adding OECD trading partners so that the U.S. market results can be viewed from a broader perspective, and by presenting annual indices for each year so that the trends can be viewed clearly and it can be verified that the particular annual cross sections chosen for analysis are not atypical (outliers) of the indices of proximate years. In addition, the presence of continuous annual observations allows us to apply a time series perspective to supplement the cross-sectional analyses.

Several theories have been advanced to explain the prevalence and proliferation of this two-way trade.

1. It is a statistical illusion, arising from the way different industries are aggregated in trade statistics.

2. It is an outgrowth of product differentiation. Obviously, if an industry produced only one standardized (and undifferentiable) product, intra-industry trade would not be likely. If, on the other hand, the industry produced a variety of differentiated products, the likelihood of such two-way trade would be enhanced.

3. The presence of scale economies enhances the likelihood of two-way trade by encouraging specialization in one or a few of the differentiated varieties within the industry.

4. Over time an increasing GNP may lead to increased two-way trade, since it signals a broadening of a country's economic base and of technological sophistication, allowing it to produce the sufficiently large and varied product mix needed for intra-industry trade. This hypothesis associates growing levels of intra-industry trade with the tendency of poor countries to diversify their productive base, and hence their exports, along with the process of development. Relative degrees of specialization are associated not with relative market forces but rather with relative levels of development. A very poor country may demonstrate a very high degree of specialization (or a very low degree of diversification) simply because its industrial infrastructure cannot support the production and export of a broad range of products and, as its economy grows and develops, it will diversify; that is, its observed level of product specialization in exports will tend to decrease. As noted by Balassa (1969), "One would expect that large countries . . . would produce a great variety of commodities and hence show relatively small differences in export performance indices."[5]

5. It is possible that the growing weight of IIT between the NICs and DCs is due to the growing vertical integration of MNCs. This would reflect shipments of components to NICs and of assembled components back to the OECD markets.

6. Increasing incomes may lead, in the case of initially poor countries, to increased IIT, following Linder's hypothesis. As per capita incomes and hence tastes of NICs tend to approximate those of rich DCs, the patterns of "representative demand" will tend to increasingly overlap, leading to increased IIT.

A set of statistical tests will be performed to assess the "fit" to the real world of the various theories outlined. We consider first the "statistical aggregation illusion." On the one hand, this argument by its very nature must, in the extreme, be true. If indeed we were able to disaggregate products to an extreme degree so that each and every time, objectively and subjectively viewed, was classified as a different product, then clearly by definition IIT would equal zero. Since this cannot be done, it always remains a possibility that cannot be empirically disproved. However, within the constraints imposed by industrial and trade data classification schemes, it has generally been demonstrated that IIT remains a factor at various levels of data aggregation. We therefore do not attempt to support or negate this argument.

The second and third arguments are standard ones typically applied to explain IIT between DCs. They would be supported if we found the coefficients of factors such as product differentiation and scale economies to be notably significant in those regressions of trade flows in which the IIT was especially important (or to increase from one consecutive time period to another in which the IIT weight tended to clearly increase as compared to those trade partner/periods in which IIT either decreased or remained fairly unchanged). For this set of tests, 36 cross-sectional regressions (4 NICs × 3 OECD markets) were run on 101 manufactured products for the time periods 1970, 1980, and 1987. The equation estimated is

$$IIT_i = a_1 + b_1 \,(\text{DIFF}) + b_2 \,(\text{SCALE}) + b_3 \,(\text{FTD})$$

where DIFF is Hufbauer's proxy for product differentiation measured as the coefficient of variation of unit values of U.S. exports; SCALE is Hufbauer's measure of scale economies, which is the slope coefficient from the logarithmic regression of value added per worker on plant size for U.S. industries in 1963; and FTD is the first-trade date, indirectly hinting at the product life-cycle stage of the product, that is, the higher the index, the "newer" and more technologically innovative the product. Table 9.5 indicates those cases in which statistically significant coefficients were found. The first column (PRD) is related to the third hypothesis above; the second (SCALE) to the fourth; and the third column (FTD) to the fifth explanation. The results are summarized in the first three columns. (IIT was later estimated with a bivariate regression using average wage as the explanatory variable; the results are summarized in the fourth column.)

The results can be interpreted two ways. On the one hand, the sparseness of significant results can be seen as failing to support the general hypothesis. Thus the intra-industry trade between NICs and OECD DC markets cannot be explained in terms of standard embodied characteristics (PRD and SCALE) or technological considerations associated with the product life cycle (FTD). This conclusion is strengthened by the observation that even in those few cases when product differentiation (PRD) *was* found to be positively significant, the scale economies measure (SCALE) was not.

On the other hand, even if the general validity of the point made in the preceding paragraph is accepted, one may still ask whether there were any particular periods and markets in which the general hypothesis is supported. The answer to this less ambitious query is that the presence of product differentiation was a significant explaining factor of IIT for Taiwan's trade with the EC in the late 1970s and late 1980s. This was true as well for Singapore's trade with the United States and with

Table 9.5 Statistically Significant Coefficients
for Regression of IIT on Product Characteristics

		PRD	SCALE	FTD	Average Wage
			South Korea		
U.S.	1966				− [a]
	1978				
	1987				
EC	1966				
	1978				
	1987				
Japan	1966	− [a]			− [b]
	1978				− [a]
	1987			+ [a]	
			Taiwan		
U.S.	1966			− [a]	
	1978			+ [a]	+ [a]
	1987			+ [b]	+ [a]
EC	1966				− [a]
	1978	+ [b]			
	1987	+ [b]			
Japan	1966				− [a]
	1978				
	1987				
			Singapore		
U.S.	1966			− [b]	
	1978				− [b]
	1987	+ [a]			− [b]
EC	1966		+ [b]		
	1978			+ [a]	− [b]
	1987	+ [b]			− [b]
Japan	1966		+ [b]		
	1978				− [b]
	1987				− [b]
			Hong Kong		
U.S.	1966			− [b]	
	1978				
	1987				
EC	1966		+ [a]		− [b]
	1978				− [b]
	1987			− [a]	− [b]
Japan	1966				− [b]
	1978				− [b]
	1987		+ [a]		− [b]

[a]Significant at the 90% level.
[b]Significant at the 95% levels.

the EC in the late 1980s. Thus at least for several individual cases, intra-industry specialization was important for NIC two-way trade with the U.S. and the EC markets.

As noted, as an economy grows, it not only attains a potential for a broad variety of production within specific industry classifications, but it also attains the technological skill to produce more innovative varieties, closer to the cutting edge of technology. This is roughly indicated by the first-date variable, FTD. The third column of Table 9.5 supports the hypothesis that this capability helped explain the growing IIT for South Korea's trade with Japan by the late 1980s, Taiwan's trade with the United States in the late 1970s and late 1980s, and Singapore's trade with the EC in the late 1970s.

A negative coefficient for FTD indicates that intra-industry trade was especially associated with more "mature," or standardized, products and varieties of products. This was found to be true for Taiwan, Singapore, and Hong Kong—all for their trade with the United States in the mid-1960s. This is a sensible result, indicating that during this period, when IIT was relatively small across the board, what little two-way trade did exist was in no way associated with technologically advanced products.

Finally, if the sixth (MNC vertical integration) hypothesis holds, then we would expect to find a significantly negative coefficient to be associated with a variable measuring relative wages for each product (industry) in the cross-sectional regressions. This is true since the decision to ship components and subassemblies from one country to another would presumably be motivated primarily by relative wage costs. The fourth column of Table 9.5 does indeed provide a large degree of support for this hypothesis. It indicates the occurrences in which b_1 in the following equation was found to be statistically significant:

$$IIT_i = a_1 + b_1 (AVWG)_i$$

where AVGW is Hufbauer's average wage of industry production workers for U.S. industries in 1961. Clearly a negative average wage was a significant explainer of IIT in many cases for each of the four NICs.[6]

A second test was carried out to examine the fifth hypothesis. The IIT indices were correlated with the MOFA variable. As noted in Chapter 7, this is the ratio of imports into the U.S. from LDCs (primarily NICs) originating from subsidiaries of U.S.-majority-owned MNCs. This particular test failed to support the hypothesis, as a positively significant correlation coefficient was discovered only for Taiwan's trade with the United States in 1987 (out of 36 cases). It is possible that the MNC vertical integration argument is not generally descriptive of the IIT observed in NIC–OECD trade relations, and it may be applicable only in a highly concentrated, small set of industries, such as transport equipment and electronics.

Finally, the last (Linder) hypothesis was examined by estimating 12 sets of time series for each of the 12 NIC–OECD market combinations:

$$IIT = a + b_1(Y_o - Y_n) + b_2(Y_n)$$

where Y_o is the per capita income of the OECD country (or group of countries) and Y_n is the per capita income of the NIC. The inference that indeed this Linder mechanism is an important factor explaining IIT trade would follow if b_1 was found to be significantly negative.

Actually the equation estimated here consists of a joint test of both the sixth (Linder) hypothesis and the fourth hypothesis (that a growing GNP provides a supply basis for greater IIT).

The results were not supportive of the Linder hypothesis. Of the 12 cases, a significantly negative coefficient (b_1) was found in only 2 cases (Taiwan–Japan and Hong Kong–EC), while significantly positive coefficients were found in 4 cases (all 3 of South Korea's trade flows and Singapore–EC). That is, in these 4 cases, higher IITs were associated with greater per capita income differences.

The second hypothesis, which corresponds to the Balassa theory of product specialization, as described earlier in this chapter, did gain fairly strong support. Of the 12 cases, 7 had a significantly positive coefficient for b_2 (with not a single significant negative coefficient).

SUMMARY

The roots of successful economic development may be sought in extent and degree of product specialization. The four NICs shared an unusually similar and uniform experience in the manner in which their respective patterns of export specialization and diversification changed over the period studied. It is argued here that these patterns may provide an important clue to why this particular group of poor countries succeeded when so many others failed (including those like the Philippines with very high levels of education and human capital endowments). Changes in the coefficient of variation of respective NIC export vectors were examined over time. Evidence supporting both the Balassa and the Ricardo effects were found, as degrees of both inter- and intra-industry specialization changed in a cyclical fashion through the period.

Measures of intra-industry trade for each NIC in each of several OECD markets were examined. Several hypotheses were forwarded to explain the relationship between the growing proportion of IIT in these countries' trade. These were then each tested statistically and verified or rejected.

Appendix Table 9.1 Intra-Industry Indices, All NICs and Markets, 1965–1990

	k_u	k_e	k_j	t_u	t_e	t_j	s_u	s_e	s_j	h_u	h_e	h_j
1965	8.6	3.7	4.3	13.1	10.2	1.5				17.4	18.5	8.1
	8.6	4.6	3.9	18.8	7.4	1.9	7.1	14.6	0.4	22.4	20.6	7.5
1967	7.6	4.6	8.8	20.1	10.0	3.8	7.3	9.6	1.2	19.6	22.6	9.9
	9.8	2.1	7.9	25.9	8.3	3.9	4.3	9.6	0.6	18.7	21.5	9.9
1969	14.2	3.0	10.8	26.1	13.1	6.0	14.7	9.4	0.7	21.5	23.4	10.1
	14.1	6.7	17.1	24.2	13.8	11.7	30.2	13.7	1.0	19.5	21.4	12.5
1971	15.8	13.4	21.8	23.2	12.9	9.3	31.9	14.7	3.3	19.2	23.8	9.7
	17.2	17.9	25.0	23.4	16.2	11.1	41.8	30.0	4.6	19.4	25.6	8.9
1973	20.0	14.4	30.0	23.0	14.5	16.3	41.0	31.3	7.2	21.6	27.3	18.1
	22.2	14.6	29.7	24.4	15.8	17.3	40.4	32.2	5.8	25.0	27.8	13.1
1975	20.7	13.5	31.3	22.5	14.5	16.3	41.1	32.3	6.6	23.0	25.2	11.9
	24.2	14.3	33.4	21.3	17.0	20.6	48.4	31.3	13.6	24.5	23.2	12.8
1977	20.4	15.9	28.1	23.7	20.0	19.2	51.3	33.4	8.6	20.9	27.5	10.6
	16.7	16.9	21.6	19.3	23.2	18.7	29.5	36.4	8.8	19.1	29.4	12.1
1979	17.0	13.2	26.3	19.9	22.4	24.0	27.2	38.5	9.4	21.8	30.3	13.6
	19.3	23.1	36.1	22.8	22.8	21.5	26.4	38.0	8.1	26.2	26.9	10.6
1981	19.7	16.1	38.8	25.5	23.4	22.5	31.8	36.0	10.8	28.3	29.4	9.7
	30.7	19.5	36.9	22.1	21.8	26.5	46.9	35.0	8.2	28.4	30.6	10.6
1983	29.0	19.6	34.0	19.7	20.9	25.0	48.7	38.6	7.9	27.0	30.2	11.2
	25.8	22.3	32.3	16.8	21.6	26.5	49.2	43.4	12.9	25.5	31.9	10.6
1985	25.0	25.2	32.5	14.9	25.4	29.8	50.5	43.0	14.5	23.6	34.3	10.1
	24.3	22.3	29.1	16.7	27.2	25.7	49.2	45.0	14.8	23.3	31.1	11.5
1987	24.1	21.6	31.3	19.1	23.9	28.0	48.3	40.4	16.3	24.8	31.4	12.1
	26.6	22.4	35.8	24.8	25.8	33.8	52.7	41.6	17.1	31.6	34.7	12.1
1989	29.3	25.9	36.8	27.0	27.6	36.4	48.9	42.2	21.6	30.4	37.3	13.7
1990	33.1	27.9	38.1	30.0	30.1	37.2	47.5	41.4	21.7	29.7	37.9	12.4

Note: k_u = Korea and trade with U.S. t_u = Taiwan and trade with U.S. s_u = Singapore and trade with U.S. h_u = Hong Kong and trade with U.S. e = EC. j = Japan.

143

NOTES

1. Balassa (1977), p. 159.

2. An illustrative example of how intra-industry production is represented by this level of disaggregation, the product "textile yarn" includes the following three-digit SITC product categories: textile yarn and thread, woven cotton fabrics, other woven fabrics, tulle lace and embroidery, special textile fabrics, and made-up articles chiefly of textile materials.

3. E.g., see Willmore (1972) on developing countries and Manrique (1987) on NICs and developed countries.

4. E.g., Bergstrand (1982, p. 50).

5. Balassa (1969, p. 107).

6. Since average wage had been found to be an important explainer of (net) export flows, one may wonder whether the findings here are merely a spurious reflection of that fact (since net exports are one term appearing in the denominator of the IIT index). The following test suggests that this is not the case. When IIT indices were correlated with trade flows for each of the 36 cases examined, they were found to be significantly and positively correlated in only 8 cases.

REFERENCES

Balassa, Bela. 1965. "Trade Liberalization and Revealed Comparative Advantage." *Manchester School of Economics and Social Studies* 33:99–123.

Balassa, Bela. 1979. "The Changing Pattern of Comparative Advantage in Manufactured Goods." *Review of Economics and Statistics* 61:259–66.

Bergstrand, J. 1982. "The Scope and Causes of Intra-Industry Trade." *New England Economic Review* 50 (September/October):36–54.

Grubel, H., and P. Lloyd. 1975. *Intra-Industry Trade: The Theory and Measurement of International Trade in Differentiated Products.* London: Macmillan.

Hufbauer, G. 1970. "The Impact of National Characteristics and Technology on the Commodity Composition of Trade in Manufactured Goods." In R. Vernon (ed.), *The Technology Factor in International Trade.* Chicago: National Bureau of Economic Research, pp. 145–232.

Linder, S. 1961. *An Essay on Trade and Transformation.* New York: John Wiley.

Manrique, Gabriel. 1987. "Intra-Industry Trade Between Developed and Developing Countries: The United States and the NICs." *Journal of Developing Areas* 22 (July):481–94.

Willmore, Larry. 1972. "Free Trade in Manufactures Among Developing Countries: The Central American Experience." *Economic Development and Cultural Change* 20, no. 4 (July):659–70.

10
The Next-Tier NICs: Tomorrow's Miracles

The rapid growth and expansion of the NICs' exports have generated provocative discussion of whether the East Asian model of development—the export-led growth strategy—could be generalized. Cline (1982) argued that the economic law of fallacy of composition would apply to any developing countries emulating the export-led growth strategies of the NICs. Given the stagnant growth of world demand for manufactured exports and the current protectionist sentiment in the world economic community, it is very unlikely that the club of export-promoting economies will find any new entrants to share the hypergrowth the NICs enjoyed in the last two decades. Ranis, on the other hand, argued that there are vital opportunities for other developing countries to follow a more open-economy approach to pursue further growth because the fallacy of composition is valid only if the volume of world trade is fixed. But in fact the growth of world trade is much more rapid than that of the world economy despite the protectionism of the industrial economies.

Recently, Love illustrated that "export performance in most countries is relatively more sensitive to domestic factors, particularly the ability to compete in world markets, than to other factors (such as market condition)"[1] and the arguments of trade pessimism therefore were not supported.

In contrast to the general policy stance adopted by Latin American countries, the ASEAN countries[2] have consciously undertaken outward-looking strategies in expanding their exports and attracting foreign investments, especially since the early 1980s. Insofar as the ASEAN countries are generally considered "quasi-NICs," "near NICs," or "next-tier NICs," an interesting question to address is whether any of the "baby tigers" are likely to become "little tigers" in the coming decade. In this chapter, we compare patterns and trends of the ASEAN trade vectors and compare them with those of the NICs. The ASEAN countries differ in many regards from the NICs. The former tend to be larger in terms of geographic size and population and tend to be relatively resource-rich. Several, notably Thailand, have enjoyed rates of economic growth which surpassed those of the NICs in the past several years and are in fact commonly regarded as likely candidates for the next tier of the NICs.

The two city-states of Hong Kong and Singapore have economic structures, both in terms of size and in terms of available resource bases, which are utterly different from those of the ASEAN countries. Therefore, this chapter focuses on a comparison of the ASEAN trade performances with those of Taiwan and Korea.[3]

A COMPARISON IN RANKINGS OF RCAS BETWEEN THE NICS AND ASEAN

The stage theory of comparative advantage (Balassa, 1977) suggests that as developing countries climb up the ladder of world trade, their export structures will become more similar to those of their predecessors. The question we asked was whether the pattern of international competitiveness, as indicated by the index of revealed comparative advantage (RCA) of each of the ASEAN countries, had grown more similar to those of the NICs over time. The relevant RCA indices were calculated for each ASEAN and NIC pair for each year from 1965 to 1990. Table 10.1 presents the (rank) correlations for each respective pair of RCA indices for each fifth year.

Using the RCA similarity criteria, we conclude that Thailand and Malaysia have more successfully emulated both Korea and Taiwan over time than have the other ASEAN countries. Relatively speaking, the export pattern in Thailand was more similar to either Korea or Taiwan than was that of Malaysia in the early 1960s. However, it is evident that Malaysia's degree of revealed comparative advantage approached those of the two NICs faster than did those of the others from the mid-1970s on.

The Philippines enjoyed an early start, as its RCA indices were highly correlated with those of the NICs in the 1960s. However, over time this relationships deteriorated and weakened, so that by the 1980s the Philippines' correlation with the NICs was relatively low. This no doubt resulted partly form the political upheavals in the late Marcos period and the 1986 revolution. Internal unrest in the Philippines substantially discouraged foreign capital inflows to that country, whereas relatively stable governments in Thailand and Malaysia attracted an enormous amount of foreign direct investment to accelerate their development. Thus by the late 1980s both Malaysia and Thailand were performing much better than the Philippines according to the RCA criteria.[4]

Indonesia is a member of OPEC. Its performance in manufactured exports tends to lag those of the other ASEAN countries. Not only did it expand its exports relatively slowly, but the changes tended to be in the "wrong" direction, as the correlation coefficients of its RCA indices with those of Korea and Taiwan declined over time. A frequently offered explanation of this highlights the official neglect exhibited by the Indonesian government in matters dealing with investment in human capital as well as the "Dutch disease" its manufacturing sectors suffered during the OPEC heyday of the 1970s, illustrating the well-known maxim that "mere" richness in resource endowments offers no guarantee of successful economic development.

An analysis of the relationships between ASEAN patterns of revealed comparative advantage with those of the two city-states, Hong Kong and Singapore,

Table 10.1　Spearman Rank Correlation Coefficient
of RCA Indices Between ASEAN and NICs in OECD

	Thailand	Malaysia	Indonesia	Philippines
	Korea with ASEAN			
1965	0.3691c	0.1883a	0.1823a	0.4426c
1970	0.2656c	0.1720a	0.0667	0.3789c
1975	0.3693c	0.3933c	0.1442	0.4101c
1980	0.3081c	0.1359	0.1303	0.3732c
1985	0.3340c	0.1788a	0.0279	0.2182b
1990	0.4684c	0.3246c	0.3402c	0.4479c
	Taiwan with ASEAN			
1965	0.3178c	0.3721c	0.3674c	0.5642c
1970	0.2349b	0.2675c	0.1214	0.3248c
1975	0.4850c	0.4425c	0.2436b	0.4904c
1980	0.5495c	0.4571c	0.3972c	0.5220c
1985	0.5799c	0.4010c	0.2129c	0.3639c
1990	0.6745c	0.4941c	0.4588c	0.6054c
	Hong Kong with ASEAN			
1965	0.3001b	0.1714a	0.2185b	0.4355c
1970	0.3846c	0.3147c	0.2312b	0.4154c
1975	0.4998c	0.4416c	0.4502c	0.4957c
1980	0.6185c	0.4397c	0.4455c	0.4058c
1985	0.5551c	0.5288c	0.2707c	0.4384c
1990	0.6662c	0.4152c	0.3170c	0.5331c
	Singapore with ASEAN			
1965	0.4191c	0.5342c	0.7093c	0.3941c
1970	0.4989c	0.5192c	0.4545c	0.4991c
1975	0.4450c	0.5374c	0.4166c	0.3433c
1980	0.5451c	0.6252c	0.4784c	0.3085c
1985	0.3796c	0.4869c	0.1572c	0.3376c
1990	0.5430c	0.6129c	0.2124b	0.4329c

[a]Significant at the 90% level.
[b]Significant at the 95% level.
[c]Significant at the 99% level.

leads to similar conclusions. Over time the export structures in Thailand and Malaysia became increasingly similar to the export-oriented economies of Hong Kong and Singapore, whereas those of the Philippines and Indonesia failed to consistently "climb the ladder" to find their place among the NICs of the future.

If the NICs are considered the moving target for the ASEAN countries, then it would be interesting to know if ASEAN has moved closer to the NICs over time. To verify the lead–lag hypothesis, we compared the Spearman rank correlation coefficients between the RCA indices of the ASEAN in 1990 and the indices of the NICs in each year for the entire period. The results are reported in Table 10.2.

One way to summarize the results is to examine the rankings of the ASEAN 1990 RCA indices' correlations with each of the respective NIC 1990 RCAs. The ASEAN country whose 1990 RCA pattern was most closely correlated with a NIC's pattern

Table 10.2 Spearman Correlations Between ASEAN
1990 RCA Indices and Those of NICs in Selected Years

	Thailand	Malaysia	Indonesia	Philippines
Korea with 1990 ASEAN				
1965	0.3012c	0.2094b	0.3275c	0.4208c
1970	0.4391c	0.3776c	0.4789c	0.4877c
1975	0.5239c	0.4148c	0.4473c	0.5556c
1980	0.4377c	0.3165c	0.4131c	0.4897c
1985	0.4915c	0.3310c	0.3424c	0.4838c
1990	0.4684c	0.3246c	0.3402c	0.4479c
Taiwan with 1990 ASEAN				
1965	0.3788c	0.3393c	0.4647c	0.4500c
1970	0.6149c	0.4792c	0.4544c	0.6350c
1975	0.7170c	0.5114c	0.5072c	0.6372c
1980	0.7249c	0.5322c	0.5227c	0.6013c
1985	0.6940c	0.5013c	0.4937c	0.5768c
1990	0.6745c	0.4941c	0.4588c	0.6054c
Hong Kong with 1990 ASEAN				
1965	0.5998c	0.3804c	0.4290c	0.5027c
1970	0.6089c	0.3782c	0.3747c	0.5862c
1975	0.5839c	0.3227c	0.2971c	0.5053c
1980	0.6357c	0.3981c	0.3316c	0.5820c
1985	0.5074c	0.3769c	0.2729c	0.5311c
1990	0.6662c	0.4152c	0.3170c	0.5331c
Singapore with 1990 ASEAN				
1965	−0.0080	−0.0654	−0.0387	−0.0478
1970	0.4961c	0.3690c	0.2469b	0.3880c
1975	0.5736c	0.3883c	0.2175b	0.3608c
1980	0.6439c	0.5097c	0.2522b	0.4180c
1985	0.5020c	0.5029c	0.1982b	0.4217c
1990	0.5430c	0.6129c	0.2124b	0.4329c

aSignificant at the 90% level.
bSignificant at the 95% level.
cSignificant at the 99% level.

of that year may be considered to be a leader in the "race" to emulate that particular
NIC's export success pattern. For example, in terms of emulating Korea the ranking
from high to low is Thailand, Philippines, Indonesia, and Malaysia. When we add
up the rankings of each ASEAN country for all four NICs we reach the following
(cumulative) rankings:

Thailand   5
Philippines   9
Malaysia   11
Indonesia   15

From this one can identify Thailand as being the clear leader, Indonesia the clear
lagger, and the other two close to one another in the intermediate position.

Another way to analyze the results summarized in Table 10.2 is to note that in the case of each and every ASEAN country, the pattern of revealed comparative advantage in the late 1980s was most closely correlated with a lagged, or past, pattern of each of the NICs. By noting the nature of these lags, one can rank the ASEAN countries in terms of their success in emulating the NICs. Relative to Korea, the 1990 RCA patterns of Thailand, Malaysia, and the Philippines were most closely related to Korea's RCA of 1975. Indonesia lagged behind them, being most closely correlated with Korea's RCA of 1970. The same pattern is evident relative to Taiwan, except that this time a wider divergence between the ASEAN performance is revealed. Whereas Thailand and Malaysia are most closely correlated with Taiwan's 1980 pattern, the Philippines's 1990 pattern was most closely similar to Taiwan's export pattern of 1975. With respect to Singapore, Indonesia's pattern of comparative advantage was not significantly correlated with Singapore's for any of the years. In general, Thailand and Malaysia tie for first place in terms having their most recently available RCA indices most highly correlated with more recent NIC RCAs. The Philippines occupies an intermediate position, and Indonesia lags them all.

Thus the foregoing analyses concur: Thailand is leading and Indonesia is clearly lagging in the race to become tomorrow's NICs. The (intermediate) relative positions of the Philippines and Malaysia are reversed from one analysis to the other. When one considers the degree to which the 1990 RCA patterns of the ASEAN countries were correlated with the 1980 NIC patterns, the Philippines is ranked somewhat higher than Malaysia. When one identifies the recency of the NIC RCA pattern with which each ASEAN country's 1990 pattern is most closely correlated, the Philippines is ranked somewhat lower. This suggests that Malaysia has recently demonstrated a relatively rapid "spurt" in the race to emulate the NICs but has yet to overcome the Philippines, which had the early lead.

A close examination demonstrates that the front runner, Thailand, moved closer to Korea and Taiwan in the period immediately after the first energy crisis but has since fallen back. This pattern highlights the "flying geese," or "moving target," nature of the race. Though the ASEAN countries are rapidly expanding their manufactured exports, and rapidly effecting compositional shifts in their export product compositions, so are the NICs (in particular Taiwan and Korea). The NICs demonstrated a spurt of growth and change in the immediate aftermath of the first energy crisis, and, expectedly, the similarity of their RCA indices with those of the ASEAN countries' indices dropped significantly in the 1980s.

DYNAMIC GROWTH AND TRADE DIVERSIFICATION

The dynamic trade expansion in ASEAN countries could be assessed by comparing the respective Spearman rank coefficients of RCA indices in 1990 and previous years. If a country has been undergoing rapid dynamic changes in its industrialization and export structures, then its correlation coefficients of RCA indices in 1990 would be dissimilar with those in the early period. The more rapid the dynamic changes in an economy, the less significant the RCA index between the two time intervals.

By comparing each country's RCA index in 1990 with those of previous years (Table 10.3) we note that ASEAN countries had substantial changes in the pattern of their revealed comparative advantage in manufactured exports. Malaysia and Indonesia experienced the most profound compositional shifts in its pattern of comparative advantage. Their 1990 patterns were not even significantly correlated with their respective patterns in 1965. As noted previously, while both countries certainly demonstrate the most dynamic and thorough change in their respective export patterns, they still lag the other ASEAN countries (compared to NIC RCA patterns). Clearly their transformation began later, and the economic distance to be bridged to typical NIC export patterns was relatively larger, due to the predominance of their resource-based export compositions.

Relatively speaking, Thailand's export structural shift was more dynamic than that of the Philippines. The Spearman rank correlation coefficient of RCA indices between 1990 and 1965 in Thailand was only 0.22, whereas the counterpart in the Philippines was 0.27. This finding is consistent with our earlier conclusion that Thailand's export structure had caught up more conclusively with NIC patterns than had that of the Philippines. If the trend of the 1980s continues in the next decade, Thailand and Malaysia would seem to be more likely candidates to be next-tier NICs than either Indonesia or the Philippines.

As discussed in Balassa (1979), the degree of industrialization and trade diversification in a country can be represented by the standard deviation and coefficients of variation of its RCA indices over time. Other things being equal, the more highly industrialized the country, the more diversified its export composition will be. Hence the shrinking of the standard deviation of RCA indices over time can illustrate the degree of industrialization and trade diversification.

Examining the figures of coefficients of variation of RCA indices in Table 10.4 one can find that all ASEAN countries have undergone substantial export diversification in the last two and half decades.[5] The coefficient of variation of RCA indices in Thailand dropped from 2.96 in 1965 to 2.40 in 1990. A similar trend is found in the coefficient of variation of RCA indices for Malaysia, dropping from 3.09 to 1.96 in the same period. For the Philippines it declined from 5.48 to 1.92, and for Indonesia it dropped from 5.66 to 4.67.

Table 10.3 Spearman Rank Correlation Coefficient Between 1990 RCA Indices and RCAs—Those of Individual ASEAN Countries in Specific Years

	Thailand	Malaysia	Indonesia	Philippines
1965	0.2248[c]	0.1363	0.1159	0.2666[c]
1970	0.3919[c]	0.2467[b]	0.1801[a]	0.3165[c]
1975	0.5859[c]	0.3660[c]	0.2840[c]	0.5718[c]
1980	0.7120[c]	0.5412[c]	0.4052[c]	0.6102[c]
1985	0.8180[c]	0.6728[c]	0.6567[c]	0.7866[c]
1989	0.9767[c]	0.8618[c]	0.9196[c]	0.8996[c]

[a]Significant at the 90% level.
[b]Significant at the 95% level.
[c]Significant at the 99% level.

Table 10.4 Standard Deviation (σ) and Coefficient of Variation (COV) of RCA Indices of ASEAN (weighted by product proportions)

	Thailand		Malaysia		Indonesia		The Philippines	
	σ	COV	σ	COV	σ	COV	σ	COV
1965	1.02	2.96	0.23	3.09	9.73	5.66	4.24	5.48
1970	0.75	3.00	0.84	5.95	4.55	5.80	4.31	4.38
1975	2.11	2.65	1.60	4.82	3.80	5.72	3.33	2.75
1980	1.62	2.23	1.20	3.97	1.84	3.12	2.46	2.85
1985	1.96	2.14	1.25	3.11	4.93	4.95	1.83	2.21
1990	2.75	2.40	1.14	1.96	5.75	4.67	1.75	1.92

Comparison of ASEAN patterns shows that the most dramatic change is the Philippine's. In 1965 it had the second highest coefficient of variation (5.48), indicating a relatively high degree of specialization exceeded only by Indonesia). By 1990 this measure dropped to 1.92, the lowest of all ASEAN countries, indicating a relatively advanced degree of manufactured export diversification. Indonesia tended to remain highly specialized. Its coefficient of variation was the highest of the ASEAN countries in 1965, and it remained highest in 1990.

Since 1970 Malaysia has demonstrated a clear tendency toward diversification of its export base (continually falling coefficients of variation over this time period). If one were to interpret export diversification as indirect evidence of economic growth (the Belassa model), then Malaysia and the Philippines clearly lead in the next-tier NIC race.

SUMMARY

ASEAN countries have shifted to outward-looking growth strategies by substantially expanding and diversifying their manufactured exports to the OECD market. Analysis of these countries' indices of revealed comparative advantage over time, and comparison with those of the NICs at various points in time, as well as analysis of the respective coefficients of variation of their export vectors, led to a clear conclusion that the "most likely to succeed" are Thailand and Malaysia, while the relative lagger is Indonesia, perhaps due to the "Dutch Disease" associated with her legacy of oil boom in the 1970s.

Overall, export structures in the ASEAN, except for Indonesia, have been moving closer and closer, with various speeds, to those of the NICs. But, it is important not to take the ASEAN countries as a homogeneous group in chasing the NICs. Moreover, the NICs is a moving target which has been climbing up the country's ladder of world trade even more rapidly than ASEAN.

Statistical evidences from this Chapter are that Malaysia and Thailand seem to be more likely to become the candidates of the next tier of the NICs. But, it does not imply that they will replace the export status of the NICs in the near future.

NOTES

1. Love (1984), p. 290.
2. The ASEAN countries are Indonesia, Philippines, Thailand, Malaysia, Brunei, and Singapore. In this chapter we explicitly study the first four. Singapore is analyzed separately as one of the four East Asian NICs.
3. The revealed comparative advantage methodology utilized is described in Chapter 2.
4. This was true relative to all NICs except Hong Kong. The Philippines' RCA pattern was more highly correlated with that of Hong Kong than was that of Malaysia.
5. One should note that absolute values of standard deviation of RCA also reflect the size of the economy in each country. Hence, for comparative purposes, the coefficient of variation is a superior indicator.

REFERENCES

Balassa, Bela. 1979. "The Changing Pattern of Comparative Advantage in Manufactured Goods." *Review of Economics and Statistics* 61:259–66.

Cline, William. 1982. "Can the East Asian Model of Development Be Generalized?" *World Development* 10, no. 2:81–90.

Cline, William. 1987. Reply. *World Development* 13, no. 4:547–48.

Love, J. 1984. "External Market Conditions, Competitiveness, Diversification and LDC Exports." *Journal of Development Economics* 16:279–91.

Ranis, Gustav. 1987. "Can the East Asian Model of Development Be Generalized? A Comment." *World Development* 13, no. 4:543–45.

11

Prospects in OECD Markets

The previous chapters discussed the growth and changing status of the four little tigers in world trade in the past quarter century. What follows is a summary of our principal findings.

1. The NICs have successfully penetrated the OECD markets in the last two decades or so. The U.S. market was vital to their trade growth prior to 1978. After the second energy crisis, the U.S. market maintained its importance, but Japan increased its imports of manufactured products from the NICs (especially after the yen appreciation of 1985).

2. Economic development and trade diversification have been moving hand in hand. As exports from the NICs continue to grow, the NICs have steadily diversified their export bases in the long run, though some oscillations were observed in Hong Kong and Singapore.

3. In terms of commodity composition of exports, the NICs have gradually shifted from traditional labor-intensive products to more high-technology-intensive products; especially notable are their export shares in nonelectrical machinery in the world market. Yet, due to some institutional arrangements such as MFA, several product groups in traditional labor-intensive industries are still dominant in their exports to the OECD market. The NICs still had an oligopoly in the world market in footwear and clothing products in the late 1980s.

4. While the NICs differed significantly from one another at any given point of time, all exhibited a tendency to emulate Japan. However, rather than match and replace Japan's exports in the OECD market, they have tended to complement Japan in most product lines, including traditional labor-intensive products.

5. Trade protection imposed in the OECD affected all trading partners, developed or not. Yet the NICs were able to handle the trade barriers more successfully than other developing countries by employing a two-pronged strategy. First, they tended to rapidly increase exports in the earlier period of the middle 1960s in labor-intensive product groups in which they enjoyed a distinct competitive edge. Since increased protectionism tended to be product- rather than source-specific, they managed to maintain the relatively large market shares attained in these particular markets. Second, they tended to diversify their exports both into product groups less

heavily protected and, within product groups, into product lines facing less domestic competition within OECD markets.

6. Most of the NICs have enjoyed growth in their exports relatively faster than the trend of world trade. This growth could be attributed to the right choice of export commodities, the right market destination—where demand for their exports has kept growing—or the improvements of their productivities. The NICs maintained their export growth in the late 1970s largely through propitious destination targeting and fortunate product choice. Until then, the success of their export expansions was rooted in a competitive ability to expand market shares product by product and market by market.

7. In the 1980s the success pattern employed by the NICs increasingly appeared to be adopted by countries of ASEAN, notably Thailand and Malaysia. They succeeded in replicating the outward-oriented growth patterns of the NICs. However, the "catching-up" hypothesis is generally not supported by empirical findings; there is no strong tendency of convergence between the NICs and the ASEAN countries. Presumably this is due to infrastructure and supply rigidities exhibited by the developing countries of ASEAN, and to the fact that the NICs were growing and undergoing their own rapid structural transformations during this period.

What is the scenario of the export performances of the NICs in the coming decade? Will they continue to grow and expand their exports to the OECD market in the 1990s? These questions are interesting not just for academic economists but for policymakers in the nations involved.

To present a prospective scenario of the export status of the NICs in the coming decade and beyond, it is necessary to assess the conditions of the world economy as background for the external trading environment for the NICs.

THE INTERNATIONAL ECONOMIC ENVIRONMENT: INTO THE 1990s

The following assumptions are made to project the trend of world trade in the 1990s.

1. There will be continued slow growth in the OECD countries in the 1990s. According to the *World Development Report, 1991* by the World Bank, the growth rate of GDP for members of OECD was 3.8% in the 1965–80 period but decelerated to 3% in the decade of 1980–89. Several projections, such as Project Link of the Wharton School and InterLink of the OECD, confirm that the 1990s are expected to be a decade of slow growth for the industrialized countries. A general consensus is that an average growth between 2% to 3% is expected to be the scenario for the OECD in the 1990s.

2. A continued effort to attain greater measures of trade liberalization under the auspices of the GATT is under way, despite the relatively meager results associated with the recent Uruguay round. However, tariff levels tend already to be relatively low, and it has yet to be proven that substantial nontariff barrier gains can be made in today's recessionary, protectionism-prone world environment. From the viewpoint of the NICs, the likelihood of significant trade liberalization in the near future

is dampened by such assessments as the following: "Between 1966 and 1986, the share of imports to countries that belong to the Organization for Economic Cooperation and Development (OECD) that were affected by nontariff measures is estimated to have doubled."[1]

3. In spite of the deadlock of trade negotiations under the Uruguay round, the NICs could continue to break through trade barriers in the OECD market by shifting to product lines that are less sensitive to protectionism, as they had in past decades.

4. The development of trading blocks would promote trade flows among member countries rather than for global trade flows as a whole. The U.S.–Canada Free Trade Agreement (FTA) of 1989, the economic integration of EC into a single, unified market in 1992 and beyond, and the proposed FTA among the United States, Canada, and Mexico are developments that may significantly affect the import of traditional labor-intensive products from the NICs.

5. The momentum for a Pacific economic community may continue in the 1990s (Drysdale). Yet substantial obstacles still exist in formulating a formal customs union and/or common market in the Pacific Basin (Chow, 1989a). Significant progress has been made in organizing several nongovernmental and/or quasi-governmental organizations to promote economic cooperation among the Asian Pacific countries. Presumably, more efforts will continue to be directed to expand their functions to coordinate trade and investments activities among the Pacific Basin countries. Among other intergovernmental organizations, the Asia Pacific Economic Council (APEC) may continue to handle groundwork to coordinate industrial development and trade expansion among the Asian Pacific countries. Yet intraregional trade flows within Asian Pacific countries, except trade with the United States, will still be far below trade flows between the NICs and OECD. Hence the OECD market will still remain as the major destination for the exports from the NICs.

THE MACROSTRUCTURE OF THE NICS IN THE 1990s

After more than two decades of rapid economic growth, industrial development, and trade expansion, the NICs faced the inevitable labor shortages, rising wages, and increased environmental costs in the 1980s. Moreover, continued trade surplus against the United States led to involuntary currency appreciations, particularly after the Plaza Agreement. The growth rates of the economy in the NICs decelerated in the period between 1980 and 1989. The annual growth rate of GNP was averaged between 6% and 8% in the NICs except for Korea, which had a remarkable record of 9.7%.[2] It seems that the momentum of rapid growth and export expansion in the NICs will reach a critical turning point in the coming decades.

Among other developments that may significantly hinder the export expansions in the NICs is the trend of deindustrialization. Development theory predicts that in the earlier stage of economic development, the percentage share of the manufacturing sector in total output will increase while that of the agricultural sector will decline (Chenery and Syrquin). The structural transformation model or the Chenery–Syrquin paradigm of development, is well observed in Korea and Taiwan. During this stage of development, export from the NICs will be more likely to expand because manufactured products have relatively higher income and price elasticities of demand (the Prebisch–Singer thesis) and are less sensitive to trade protection than agricultural commodities. In fact, the success story of the NICs has defeated the structuralist school of trade pessimism, which was prevalent in the 1950s and the early 1960s, especially in Latin American countries. The structural transformation from an agrarian economy to one dominated by manufactured industry in Korea and Taiwan in the last two decades or so has demonstrated that export expansion and industrialization can be moved hand in hand in the developing countries, although there are some doubt that the reciprocal causal patterns between export and industrial development (Chow, 1987) can be replicated in other developing countries. However, as an economy matures, the manufacturing share of total outputs tends to shrink while the share of services industries in the economy tends to rise at the later stage of industrialization. An empirical investigation of the industrialized countries in the 1980s revealed that there was a declining trend of the share of manufacturing sector in total GNP in most OECD countries. Records from West Germany, Japan, and other industrialized countries all revealed that there was a strong indication that as the GNP per capita passed the threshold of $5,000, the percentage share of the manufacturing sector in total GDP started to decline (Liu et al.).

Although there might not be a one-to-one relationship between the level of per capita income and the stage of deindustrialization, most of the NICs passed the likely threshold of deindustrialization in the late 1980s. Korea, which had a per capita income of $4,400 in 1989, is an exception.

As they undergo the phenomenon of deindustrialization, the two city-states of Hong Kong and Singapore and recently Taiwan have been experiencing a second stage of structural shift toward a more service-oriented economy.[3] This development would have some detrimental effects on further trade expansion from the NICs at least in the short run, because exports of service industries from the NICs have yet to develop. Meanwhile, service industries are subject to more rigid government regulations than are manufactured goods. Moreover, the NICs may have much less comparative advantage in service industries than in manufactured industries. Hence the prospective scenario of the world trade status of the NICs in the coming decade may not be that bright as it was before.

These developments are further compounded by sociopolitical environments, which may substantially affect the economic growth and trade expansion for the NICs in the coming decade. The environmental protection, labor, and democratization movements in Korea and Taiwan, as well as the outmigration from Hong Kong of professionals who are apprehensive about its return to China in 1997, would further jeopardize the investment climates and deteriorate their international competitivenesses in the 1990s.[4] Nevertheless, other developments in the NICs may have positive effects of their export growth. The process of economic liberalization, which reduces restrictions on imports; the drive for deregulation, which eliminates the price distortions; the privatization of public enterprises, which improves efficiency (Chow, 1989b); the surge of outward foreign direct investment from the NICs; and the gradual liberalization of financial markets and institutions (Chow,

1992)—all are promising developments toward more efficient and open economies in the near future.

PROJECTIONS OF EXPORT COMPETITIVENESS
TO THE YEAR 2000

Before one can make any sensible projection for the future trend of export growth in the NICs, one has to recognize the relative importance of the U.S. market to their past export performances. The legacy of U.S. aid to Korea and Taiwan in the 1950s to 1960s (through the 1970s in Korea) has contributed to their trade dependencies on the United States as the most important market for their export destination; this is not, however, the awkward situation described by dependency theorists such as Griffin and Gurley. The relative openness of the U.S. market compared with those of Japan and the EC enabled the NICs to increase the market penetration of their export commodities. By the early 1980s the U.S. market has absorbed more than one-quarter to one-third of the manufactured exports for all the NICs except Singapore, whose exports to the United States also steadily increased as a share of total exports since the early 1980s. In any event, the United States has been and still is the largest market for the exports of the NICs. It may well be argued that the macroeconomic performance and the trade policies in the United States are not only significant but indeed are critical to any evaluation of export prospects of the NICs.

To predict export performances for the NICs in the United States in the coming decade, we first evaluate the growth rates of RCA indices in each of the 13 product groups during the late 1980s as the base for projections. Since world trade in the 1970s experienced substantial dramatic shifts due to the two energy shocks, we use the five-year average in several time periods as the initial points for our projections. Exports from the NICs also underwent substantial fluctuations in the late 1980s due to the realignment of exchange rates under the Plaza Agreement. The projections in this section are to be considered baseline forecasts, given the likely developments in the international trade environment, as discussed earlier.

The forecast tables utilize the stepwise autoregressive procedure of SAS. This procedure first fits a time trend model to the series and takes the difference between each value and its respective estimated trend value. Having thus detrended the series, the remaining variation is fit using an autoregressive model. The autoregressive process is fit to the residuals of the trend model using a backward-stepping method to select parameters.

The U.S. Market

Table 11.1 illustrates the historic and forecast values of NIC exports to the United States by product category. Table 11.2 offers similar information for U.S. import shares.

From Table 11.2 it is clear that in 1990 (and as projected to 2000) the NICs do not dominate a broad range of product groups in U.S. imports. Except for several

Table 11.1 History and Forecasts of NIC Manufactured Exports to the United States (millions of dollars)

Product Group	1985	1990	1995	2000
Korea				
Chemicals	98.4	265.3	213.8	248.7
Resource-based products	484.4	542.1	690.6	807.8
Metal-based manufactures	1,323.0	1,226.0	1,687.8	2,021.1
Nonferrous metals	20.4	8.0	15.8	12.7
Textiles	327.2	490.5	507.5	580.9
Nonelectrical machinery	462.0	1,937.1	1,359.8	1,771.9
Electrical machinery	2,178.9	3,827.0	4,302.3	4,986.6
Transport equipment	78.8	1,429.8	1,631.2	1,984.3
Precision instruments	89.3	177.2	178.4	220.6
Clothing	2,482.2	3,473.6	4,089.2	4,814.3
Furniture	39.3	73.6	82.5	100.5
Footwear	1,170.4	2,630.3	2,580.7	2,902.0
Miscellaneous	1,619.6	2,541.8	2,726.2	3,598.2
Taiwan				
Chemicals	210.8	344.8	366.7	420.1
Resource-based products	1,054.2	1,067.3	1,556.8	1,894.5
Metal-based manufactures	1,277.5	1,814.0	2,148.8	2,525.7
Nonferrous metals	32.9	28.8	21.2	19.8
Textiles	389.7	462.8	551.9	650.8
Nonelectrical machinery	1,818.7	4,262.0	4,205.9	4,615.8
Electrical machinery	3,126.3	3,991.1	5,001.8	5,995.4
Transport equipment	611.3	994.8	942.9	1,156.1
Precision instruments	252.2	416.8	479.4	562.2
Clothing	2,504.2	2,578.1	3,572.9	4,341.7
Furniture	823.4	1,104.1	1,188.5	1,581.3
Footwear	1,886.8	1,533.7	2,510.5	3,119.5
Miscellaneous	3,129.0	3,893.3	5,060.0	6,128.9
Singapore				
Chemicals	66.6	385.8	187.6	221.2
Resource-based products	23.5	50.7	49.2	55.2
Metal-based manufactures	45.3	49.5	73.4	90.8
Nonferrous metals	23.6	4.6	16.5	19.5
Textiles	5.2	9.3	14.4	15.5
Nonelectrical machinery	1,181.7	4,769.6	3,940.4	4,165.5
Electrical machinery	1,601.8	2,780.7	2,970.8	3,441.7
Transport equipment	119.9	94.1	133.4	160.6
Precision instruments	70.2	118.8	121.4	136.3
Clothing	409.7	653.7	681.7	768.6
Furniture	58.8	49.2	71.7	88.5
Footwear	0.6	0.2	2.0	2.3
Miscellaneous	147.4	283.6	369.2	444.7
Hong Kong				
Chemicals	20.4	46.8	41.3	45.6
Resource-based products	227.1	208.1	296.3	360.0
Metal-based manufactures	168.0	174.3	244.4	292.9
Nonferrous metals	9.6	14.7	19.9	23.9
Textiles	173.9	227.2	257.0	296.7

Table 11.1   Continued

Product Group	1985	1990	1995	2000
Nonelectrical machinery	761.0	839.1	1,106.1	1,334.9
Electrical machinery	1,426.2	1,319.1	1,923.0	2,312.9
Transport equipment	27.3	15.4	36.3	39.5
Precision instruments	137.6	247.9	270.6	315.5
Clothing	3,537.1	4,195.7	5,033.0	5,934.4
Furniture	38.9	32.7	58.4	67.6
Footwear	106.6	115.3	155.6	188.1
Miscellaneous	2,168.3	1,903.4	2,838.9	3,423.1

traditional or labor-intensive groups, such as clothing, footwear, and electrical machinery, the shares of the U.S. import market tend to be fairly small, and they are not forecast to improve markedly during the next decade.

Product by product, one may note that Korea has the fastest growth rates in electrical machinery, nonferrous metals, and chemicals under various time horizons. With a few exceptions, Singapore enjoyed rapid growth most of the time in items like nonferrous metals, chemicals, metal manufactures, and some resource-based products. The fastest growth exports in Hong Kong are nonferrous metals, metal manufactures, footwear, and resource-based products. The growth rate of exports in Taiwan is more evenly distributed than any other NICs. By the year 2000 Taiwan will tend to be strongly competitive in products such as precision instruments, nonferrous metals, resource-based products, furniture, and textile/clothing products. Even though Taiwanese comparative advantage has shifted to some new product lines such as precision instruments and nonferrous metals, its comparative advantage in traditional product groups such as textile/clothing and furniture still remains.

One may doubt the competitive status of Taiwanese exports in textile and clothing in the future. Yet the increasing tendency for Taiwan to shift obsolete production technologies in these traditional industries to less developed areas such as the ASEAN countries and mainland China and the continued efforts to upgrade the technology for industries remaining at home have substantially enhanced Taiwanese competitiveness in these product lines. A recent estimate conducted by the Ministry of Economic Affairs on Taiwan projected that exports of textile products will reach $20 billion in the year 2000. Despite the drive of shifting toward more technology-intensive industry, textiles will still account for 15.5% of total exports and remain as one of the most important traditional exports for Taiwan in the year 2000. Singapore will maintain its international competitiveness in nonferrous metals, chemicals, and resource-based products. It seems that Singaporean comparative advantage experienced some oscillations in the 1970s and 1980s. As discussed in chapter 9, Singaporean specialization/diversification in 13 export industries experienced some oscillations between 1965 and 1987. There may well be another cycle of trade specialization in Singapore by the year 2000. The pattern of Hong Kong's comparative advantage is less clear than that of other NICs. Hong Kong has a strong comparative position in clothing, furniture, and some miscellaneous products. The ambiguity of Hong Kong's comparative advantage in the U.S. market is com-

Table 11.2 History and Forecasts of U.S. Import Market
to the Year 2000 (%)

Product Group	1985	1990	1995	2000
Korea				
Chemicals	0.62	1.08	1.13	1.35
Resource-based products	2.49	2.05	2.57	2.74
Metal-based manufactures	7.46	6.26	9.81	11.58
Nonferrous metals	0.28	0.08	0.38	0.43
Textiles	6.58	7.31	9.37	11.43
Nonelectrical machinery	1.22	2.80	2.53	3.33
Electrical machinery	6.42	6.81	10.04	11.77
Transport equipment	0.12	1.75	2.13	2.50
Precision instruments	1.68	1.73	2.86	3.46
Clothing	15.31	12.96	19.18	22.67
Furniture	1.05	1.36	2.15	2.52
Footwear	19.17	26.27	31.95	38.47
Miscellaneous	6.20	6.65	9.55	11.08
Taiwan				
Chemicals	1.32	1.40	1.81	2.08
Resource-based products	5.42	4.04	7.11	8.16
Metal-based manufactures	7.20	9.26	8.12	13.74
Nonferrous metals	0.45	0.29	0.42	0.48
Textiles	7.84	6.90	9.69	11.84
Nonelectrical machinery	4.80	6.16	7.39	9.01
Electrical machinery	9.21	7.11	11.08	13.31
Transport equipment	0.96	1.22	1.45	1.77
Precision instruments	4.75	4.06	7.31	9.03
Clothing	15.45	9.61	16.69	20.91
Furniture	22.09	20.41	31.81	38.91
Footwear	30.91	15.35	38.98	47.33
Miscellaneous	11.97	10.18	18.47	22.16
Singapore				
Chemicals	0.42	1.57	0.93	1.06
Resource-based products	0.12	0.19	0.17	0.19
Metal-based manufactures	0.25	0.25	0.43	0.50
Nonferrous metals	0.33	0.05	0.20	0.24
Textiles	0.10	0.14	0.25	0.28
Nonelectrical machinery	3.12	6.90	6.68	7.50
Electrical machinery	4.72	4.95	7.64	8.79
Transport equipment	0.19	0.12	0.20	0.24
Precision instruments	1.32	1.14	1.65	1.93
Clothing	2.20	2.44	3.02	3.38
Furniture	1.72	0.91	1.91	2.56
Footwear	0.01	0.00	0.06	0.06
Miscellaneous	0.73	0.74	1.36	1.58
Hong Kong				
Chemicals	0.13	0.19	0.19	0.20
Resource-based products	1.17	0.79	1.29	1.47
Metal-based manufactures	0.95	0.89	1.24	1.37
Nonferrous metals	0.13	0.15	0.22	0.27

Table 11.2 Continued

Product Group	1985	1990	1995	2000
Textiles	3.50	3.38	3.74	3.63
Nonelectrical machinery	2.01	1.21	2.49	3.11
Electrical machinery	3.94	2.35	2.49	1.79
Transport equipment	0.04	0.02	0.00	0.00
Precision instruments	2.59	2.42	3.61	4.08
Clothing	21.82	15.65	17.92	18.29
Furniture	1.04	0.60	0.30	0.00
Footwear	1.75	1.15	1.70	1.83
Miscellaneous	8.29	4.98	6.12	5.34

pounded by the increasing resource flows between Hong Kong and mainland China. There has been a significant trend of economic integration between Hong Kong and Canton province, the adjacent area in China, especially after the late 1980s. Presumably, more and more economic integration between Hong Kong and China will further reinforce Hong Kong's export competitiveness in various export industries if China honors its agreement to retain the capitalistic economic system of Hong Kong after 1997.

The EC Market

The European market is likely to become increasingly significant for the NICs' exports in the coming decade. The integration of the EC into a single, unified market in 1992 would make it more attractive for the NICs. It is also likely that those product lines for which the NICs already have a toehold in the EC will experience accelerating growth rates due to the expected market expansion after integration. Since there are many product lines in which the NICs do not export any significant amount to the EC, the EC market projections are subject to more uncertainties than are U.S. market projections.

Table 11.3 illustrates the historic and forecast values of EC-bound exports by product category.

The Japanese Market

As discussed in chapter 4, Korea and Taiwan gradually focused on Japan's market through the 1980s. This trend was aggravated in the mid-1980s. On the one hand, the yen started to appreciate right after the Plaza Agreement. On the other hand, the persistent trade surplus in Korea and Taiwan against the United States caused Washington to put strong pressure on those countries to reduce their exports to the United States. Despite the rigid market structure in Japan's import–export trade, some of the NICs, notably Korea and Taiwan, have increased their exports to Japan's market.

Table 11.4 presents the forecasts to the Japan market. As may be noted, Japan tended to be a more important market than either the United States or the EC for NIC products at the bottom of the production process such as chemicals, resource-based products, metal-based products, and nonferrous metals. For more sophisti-

Table 11.3 History and Forecasts of NIC Manufactured Exports to the EC (millions of dollars)

Product Group	1985	1990	1995	2000
Korea				
Chemicals	46.4	171.4	120.7	140.2
Resource-based products	95.8	242.0	277.6	336.4
Metal-based manufactures	89.3	304.9	295.3	347.7
Nonferrous metals	1.7	6.4	4.2	4.7
Textiles	166.1	398.3	333.9	481.0
Nonelectrical machinery	200.7	791.4	482.4	747.3
Electrical machinery	364.3	1,893.8	1,600.2	1,742.2
Transport equipment	106.9	1,497.6	203.2	244.5
Precision instruments	21.9	97.5	84.8	92.0
Clothing	736.0	1,221.4	1,799.2	2,114.1
Furniture	0.8	7.1	5.5	7.6
Footwear	153.5	679.3	524.4	598.2
Miscellaneous	333.1	1,228.8	1,104.0	1,402.2
Taiwan				
Chemicals	48.8	344.8	133.2	148.7
Resource-based products	197.5	468.8	500.5	608.2
Metal-based manufactures	138.0	622.7	542.6	597.6
Nonferrous metals	1.1	7.8	4.3	5.0
Textiles	152.5	421.7	378.5	434.3
Nonelectrical machinery	387.8	2,754.0	1,929.6	2,028.0
Electrical machinery	543.3	2,046.8	1,748.4	1,963.8
Transport equipment	30.0	550.7	253.1	294.4
Precision instruments	40.4	224.8	185.9	197.3
Clothing	309.6	520.5	700.5	830.7
Furniture	34.8	141.6	116.1	154.9
Footwear	235.8	441.7	538.2	642.8
Miscellaneous	615.1	1,841.1	1,699.3	2,125.5
Singapore				
Chemicals	68.3	156.8	126.4	152.5
Resource-based products	54.2	135.4	137.9	177.2
Metal-based manufactures	32.9	84.7	78.6	87.8
Nonferrous metals	7.7	26.6	26.7	32.0
Textiles	4.7	20.2	22.6	25.5
Nonelectrical machinery	371.4	1,970.8	1,271.6	1,372.3
Electrical machinery	536.2	2,037.3	1,573.4	1,800.3
Transport equipment	30.3	47.0	39.3	46.8
Precision instruments	15.0	68.2	56.8	61.2
Clothing	47.5	248.3	182.7	286.2
Furniture	1.2	22.1	11.1	20.9
Footwear	0.5	10.2	3.7	4.4
Miscellaneous	138.7	775.6	461.9	543.1
Hong Kong				
Chemicals	9.0	55.0	43.9	46.4
Resource-based products	95.0	311.7	255.4	321.0
Metal-based manufactures	78.6	155.6	176.6	205.5
Nonferrous metals	6.5	11.0	45.9	43.4
Textiles	118.2	198.1	219.0	249.0
Nonelectrical machinery	297.0	769.8	644.6	730.8

Table 11.3 Continued

Product Group	1985	1990	1995	2000
Electrical machinery	412.9	1,310.9	1,249.8	1,436.1
Transport equipment	7.3	39.1	24.3	28.9
Precision instruments	71.1	251.6	235.8	260.5
Clothing	1,459.4	3,307.2	3,123.1	4,031.0
Furniture	7.5	17.9	19.0	23.3
Footwear	48.6	64.5	77.2	87.4
Miscellaneous	907.2	2,268.4	2,080.0	2,732.7

cated products, such as nonelectrical machinery, Japan's market was notably smaller. These relative weights of the Japanese market are projected to remain roughly the same in the next decade, though in some more advanced product groups, such as electrical machinery, Japan is forecast to increase its NIC-sourced imports considerably. It should be noted that in several product groups, NIC exports to Japan already comprise a high proportion of Japan's total imports of those products, so that there is little room for increased market shares in these import markets. For example, in 1990 Korea supplied 24.6% of all of Japan's metal manufactures (and Taiwan another 8%). Clothing imports into Japan are also largely comprised of NIC-sourced products. In 1990, some 28% came from Korea, 5% from Taiwan, and another 6% from Hong Kong. Footwear is another such product, with 33% of Japan's imports originating in Korea.

Quite unexpectedly, the comparative advantage of Korea in Japan's market would fall on those product groups such as resource-based product, nonelectrical machinery, furniture, clothing, precision instruments, and miscellaneous manufactures under various assumptions. There was also a clear tendency for Korean footwear to become more competitive in the second half of the 1980s. Taiwanese exports of resource-based products, nonferrous metals, transport equipment, furniture, clothing, and miscellaneous manufactures would seem likely to gain substantial comparative advantage in the coming decade.

Singapore would maintain comparative advantage in chemicals, nonferrous metals, nonelectrical machinery, and furniture in Japan's market. For precision instruments, Singapore would lose its comparative advantage under all sets of projections. The export pattern of Hong Kong in Japan's market seems to be more stable in terms of its comparative advantage. Hong Kong would keep its comparative advantage in nonferrous metals, transport equipment, clothing, and miscellaneous manufactures under any projections.

PROJECTIONS OF NIC EXPORT COMPETITIVENESS IN THE OECD MARKET

Several summarizing observations may now be made. Tables 11.1 through 11.4 show in detail the expectations we have concerning the forecast export expansion of the four NICs in each of the three major OECD markets. Naturally, these may be affected by many unforeseen political as well as economic developments. Thus it is

Table 11.4 History and Forecasts of NIC Manufactured Exports to Japan (millions of dollars)

Product Group	1985	1990	1995	2000
Korea				
Chemicals	202.2	560.1	552.8	640.1
Resource-based products	166.6	522.6	436.0	568.3
Metal-based manufactures	438.6	1,550.2	1,219.5	1,639.6
Nonferrous metals	16.6	105.0	106.9	125.4
Textiles	318.4	535.2	686.5	805.3
Nonelectrical machinery	56.8	485.5	330.6	341.0
Electrical machinery	321.8	1,212.4	828.7	1,188.7
Transport equipment	5.3	84.4	58.9	65.0
Precision instruments	23.1	80.8	66.2	73.6
Clothing	619.9	2,410.0	1,823.3	2,726.5
Furniture	26.7	122.6	88.0	122.2
Footwear	122.4	432.1	407.8	462.5
Miscellaneous	246.3	1,075.5	788.0	1,081.1
Taiwan				
Chemicals	118.2	312.5	305.3	350.4
Resource-based products	116.1	366.9	341.9	423.8
Metal-based manufactures	166.1	504.2	421.2	476.2
Nonferrous metals	26.7	174.3	108.2	152.0
Textiles	111.1	328.8	293.8	376.8
Nonelectrical machinery	90.2	544.5	355.2	444.9
Electrical machinery	306.6	1,096.6	797.4	1,082.3
Transport equipment	10.1	180.2	121.3	126.0
Precision instruments	35.1	110.5	77.2	115.0
Clothing	253.8	439.0	609.0	766.9
Furniture	128.3	284.1	272.6	382.7
Footwear	106.7	257.4	242.8	322.7
Miscellaneous	304.2	1,064.1	859.8	1,192.3
Singapore				
Chemicals	150.4	444.7	424.4	471.8
Resource-based products	7.7	58.5	29.4	34.7
Metal-based manufactures	5.5	37.1	24.8	36.7
Nonferrous metals	5.6	26.1	16.0	17.7
Textiles	4.9	11.2	11.6	14.9
Nonelectrical machinery	69.7	393.6	226.2	257.5
Electrical machinery	91.9	398.6	308.7	332.5
Transport equipment	5.7	6.1	22.6	26.1
Precision instruments	3.7	27.4	14.7	18.7
Clothing	1.0	10.0	5.5	6.3
Furniture	1.7	42.2	21.1	29.0
Footwear	0.3	2.6	1.6	1.8
Miscellaneous	36.1	151.3	113.9	123.8
Hong Kong				
Chemicals	27.6	42.3	44.8	52.4
Resource-based products	31.3	203.8	142.5	159.3
Metal-based manufactures	21.9	60.4	53.3	67.5
Nonferrous metals	2.6	5.9	4.8	5.5
Textiles	17.8	38.2	44.8	52.0

Table 11.4 Continued

Product Group	1985	1990	1995	2000
Nonelectrical machinery	19.1	111.0	87.1	92.6
Electrical machinery	26.4	139.1	91.6	126.8
Transport equipment	0.1	7.5	8.7	10.3
Precision instruments	7.6	41.3	26.2	29.1
Clothing	237.5	541.5	588.2	687.8
Furniture	3.2	7.7	11.2	11.4
Footwear	0.3	1.8	1.7	2.0
Miscellaneous	162.0	535.2	434.9	571.3

possible that the breakup of the former Soviet Union may create unforeseen international trade and investment patterns that will affect the results here. We have here forecast a slight increase in Korea's market share in the OECD markets for this product group. However, it is always possible that a concerted effort in the ASEAN countries, such as Thailand, may displace Korea from its position in this product group. The forecasts as presented in the preceding tables are merely the technical projection of autoregressive patterns, buttressed by our judgment, given the world economic environment as viewed today.

In Taiwan, it is likely that the exports of metal manufactures, nonelectrical machinery, furniture, footwear, and miscellaneous manufactures will tend to capture larger OECD import market shares over the coming decade. In other product groups, such as electrical machinery and clothing, in the entire OECD market, Taiwan may face strong challenges after 1995 despite its ability to maintain comparative advantage in some submarkets, such as the United States.

Hong Kong has a consistent trend of growth in comparative advantage in those product groups such as electrical machinery, precision instruments, clothing, and miscellaneous products. Singapore's exports in nonelectrical machinery have grown steadily. For electrical machinery and chemicals, Singapore's comparative advantages seem to be less stable than other product groups. If the OECD market remains open to the NICs in the coming decade, then the NICs will continue to penetrate in traditional product lines such as the clothing and footwear products as well as in some more technology-intensive ones. If the growth of export performance (as reflected by their respective RCA indices) for the NICs in the coming decade follows the same trend as the period between 1970–74 and 1985–87, then one can expect that electrical and nonelectrical machinery will be the common items that show strong comparative advantage for the NICs in the OECD market. Clothing is another item for which all the NICs except Singapore will maintain a comparative advantage. Strong comparative advantage in precision instruments will be maintained by Hong Kong and Taiwan, whereas footwear will be strong for Korea and Taiwan. Korea is the only candidate that has a strong potential to develop a comparative advantage in transport equipment. But if a more recent trend in growth rate (i.e., in the period between 1980–84 and 1985–87) is more likely to be replicated in the near future, then the export patterns would become more divergent among the NICs. Korea would seem to perform extremely well in nonelectrical machinery, electrical machinery, transport, footwear, clothing, and miscellaneous products.

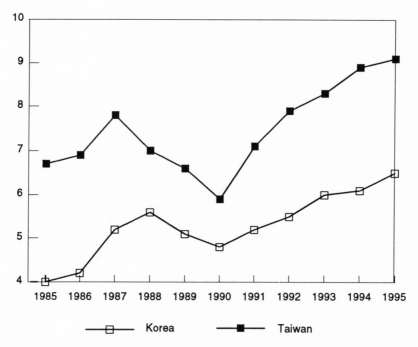

Figure 11.1   Historic and forecast shares of Taiwan and Korea in U.S. import market.

Taiwan would maintain strong comparative advantage in metal manufactures, non-ferrous metals, nonelectrical machinery, footwear, furniture, and miscellaneous products. Singapore would have strong comparative advantage in nonelectrical machinery, chemicals, and metal manufactures. Hong Kong would uphold its comparative advantage in precision instruments, electrical machinery, clothing, and miscellaneous products. Therefore, exports of traditional products will still account for substantial shares in total exports from the NICs even though they will continue to shift to more high-technology-intensive products in the coming decades. But this prognostication is not totally unreasonable in view of the fact that Japan's exports of traditional labor-intensive products still gained substantial market share in the United States after the mid-1970s.

In general, we forecast that the four NICs will tend to continue increasing their overall market shares in the OECD markets. These forecasts are summarized in Figures 11.1 and 11.2, which illustrate the projected shares of each of the NICs in the U.S. market to the year 1995.

TOWARD FULL MEMBERSHIP IN THE OECD COUNTRIES

If indeed the coming decade sees a continuation of the trade and income growth of the four NICs, then an interesting question arises: At what stage of economic

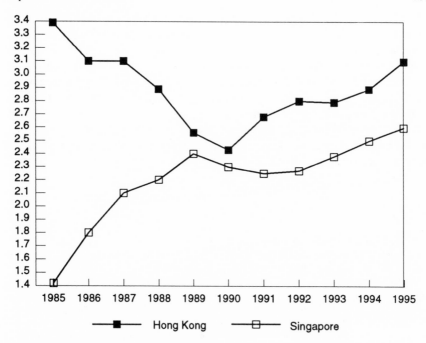

Figure 11.2 Historic and forecast shares of Singapore and Hong Kong in U.S. market.

development should these countries be considered "developed" or "industrialized"? The NICs today are universally acknowledged as having graduated from the LDC or developing class of countries. It is therefore sensible to attempt to assess the likelihood of these countries being accepted as full-fledged members of the OECD.

The criterion for being an industrialized country varies in accordance with different perceptions of economists. Lawerence Klein used the GDP per capita in Italy as a benchmark to qualify Japan's membership status in OECD; Japan reached Italy's level of per capita GDP in 1963, prior to admittance to the OECD. What would the prospects be for Korea and Taiwan to become OECD members if one adopts the income of Italy or Japan as the relevant criterion?

Based on a 2% growth in per capita income in the United States and Italy and a 5% growth in per capita income in Taiwan and Korea, Klein concluded that "Taiwan falls just short of the Italian figure 6691, measured in international prices of 1975, vs. 6805, where Korea is a bit lower at 5325. At about 6 or 7% growth, then, South Korea could easily qualify too."[5] Since Taiwan was able to keep its growth rate above 6% in the 1987–90 period[6] and is expected to maintain a projected rate of growth between 6% and 8% in the next decade, one can reasonably assume that Taiwan will be qualified as a full member of OECD by the year of 2000. Similarly, Singapore and Hong Kong's per capita incomes are within reasonable striking distance of the threshold.

It is likely that the major hurdles these countries will face in their bid for membership in IMF, GATT, OECD, and other international organizations as full-fledged developed, industrialized countries are political.[7] Given political realities in the world community, Taiwan's bid must contend with the objections and interests of the People's Republic of China. South Korea's attempt to gain the full recognition due its economic attainments and position must contend with the objections and interests of North Korea, which may become less difficult to overcome now that both have been admitted to U.N. membership. Hong Kong is technically not a country and is not likely to become one in the foreseeable future. Only Singapore faces no clear political problem.

NOTES

1. World Bank, *World Development Report, 1991*, p. 8.
2. See World Bank, *World Development Report, 1991*, p. 9, and *Taiwan Statistical Data Book, 1990*, p. 13.
3. In fact, some economists in Taiwan have recently expressed concern about the problem of "Dutch disease." See Schive (1991).
4. It is clear that political stability is crucial to growth and development of any country, including of course the NICs. To some extent, all the Asian NICs, except perhaps Singapore, face recognized political uncertainties in the 1990s: possible reunification of North and South Korea; the evolving normalization of the relationship between Beijing and Taipei; and the restoration of Hong Kong to China after 1997. All involve significant uncertainties in the near to midrange future. Our projections are based on the assumption that these developments would not dramatically affect their trade performances in the coming decade.
5. Klein (1987), pp. 7–8.
6. *Taiwan Statistical Data Book*, 1991, p. 23.
7. See Ramon Myers, "Taiwan Deserves to Join the World Community." *Asian Wall Street Journal*, Dec. 21, 1989, pp. 5–6.

REFERENCES

Balassa, Bela. 1989. *Comparative Advantage, Trade Policy and Economic Development*. New York: New York University Press, pp. 1–80.
Chenery, H. B., and Moises Syrquin. 1975. *Patterns of Development, 1950–70*. London: Oxford University Press.
Chow, Peter C. Y. 1987. "Causality Between Export Growth and Industrial Development: Empirical Evidence from the NICs." *Journal of Development Economics* 26:55–63.
———. 1989a. "Economic Integration in the Pacific Basin Countries." In Bernard T. K. Joei (ed.), *From Pacific Region Toward Pacific Community*. Taipei: Center for Area Studies, Tamkank University, pp. 331–48.
———. 1989b. "Economic Liberalization in Taiwan and Its Implications for Pacific Development." In Bernard T. K. Joei (ed.), *Taiwan in Transition*. Taipei: Center for Area Studies, Tamkang University, pp. 331–48.
———. 1992. "Financial Liberalization and Macro-Stability in a Small Open Economy: Taiwan's Experience in a Global Perspective." *Proceedings of International Seminar on Economics and Finance*. Tokyo Metropolitan University, Tokyo, Japan, May, pp. 181–205.
Drysdale, Peter. 1985. "Building the Foundations of a Pacific Economic Community." In Toshio

Shishido and Ryuzo Sato (eds.), *Economic Policy and Development: New Perspectives*. London: Croom Helm, pp. 46–58.

Griffin, Keith, and John Gurley. 1985. "Radical Analysis of Imperialism, the Third World, and the Transition to Socialism: A Survey Article." *Journal of Economic Literature:* 1089–1143.

Klein, Lawerence R. 1987. "Asia-Pacific Economies: Challenges and Prospects." In M. Dutta (ed.), *Asia-Pacific Economies: Promises and Challenges,* Vol. 6, Part A. Greenwich, Conn.: JAI Press.

Liu, Tai-Yin, Craig Wu, Pon-Chin Chen, and Hwi-Chin Lee. 1988. *Report on Manufacturing Development Strategy*. Taipei: Taiwan Institute for Economic Research.

Myers, R. "Taiwan Deserves to Join the World Community." *Asian Wall Street Journal,* Dec. 21, 1989, pp. 5–6.

OECD. *The International Macroeconomic Model–Interlink*. Paris: OECD, various issues.

Schive, Chi. 1991. "How did Taiwan Solve Its Dutch Disease Problem?" Paper presented at the fifth Biennial Conference on U.S.–Asia Economic Relations, sponsored by the American Committee on Asian Economic Studies in cooperation with Tokai University. Tokyo, Japan, June 20–22.

World Bank. 1991. *World Development Report*. Washington, D.C., and London: Oxford University Press.

Index